AN
TRACKS
ID
& TECHNIQUES

Flame Lily Press
P.O. Box 229
Falmouth
Cornwall
TR11 5SS
www.shadowhawk.co.uk
info@shadowhawk.co.uk

First Published 2007

10 9 8 7 6 5 4 3 2 1

Reproduction by St Ives Roch

ISBN 978-0-9554348-0-8

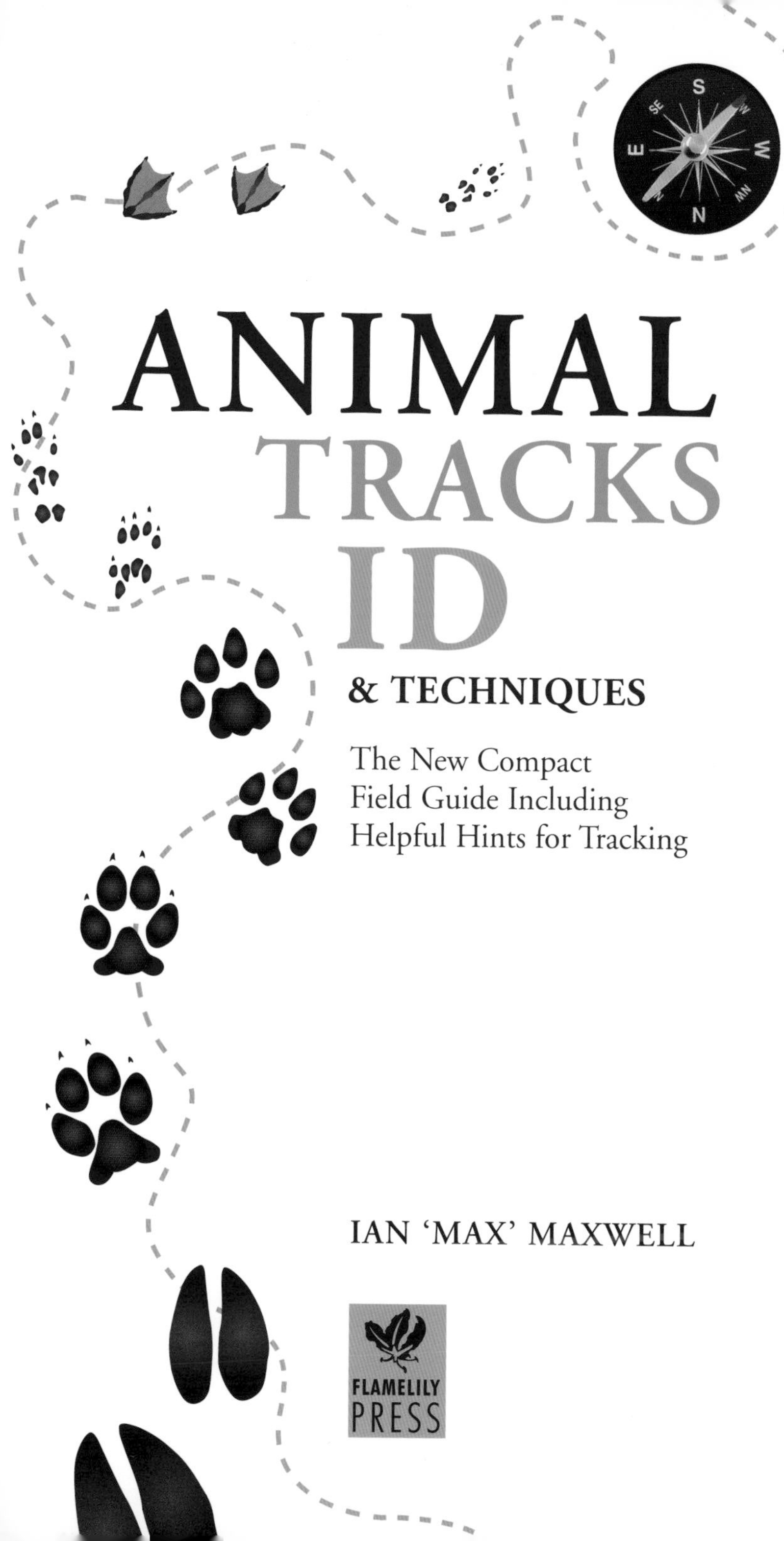

ANIMAL TRACKS ID

& TECHNIQUES

The New Compact
Field Guide Including
Helpful Hints for Tracking

IAN 'MAX' MAXWELL

FLAMELILY
PRESS

CONTENTS

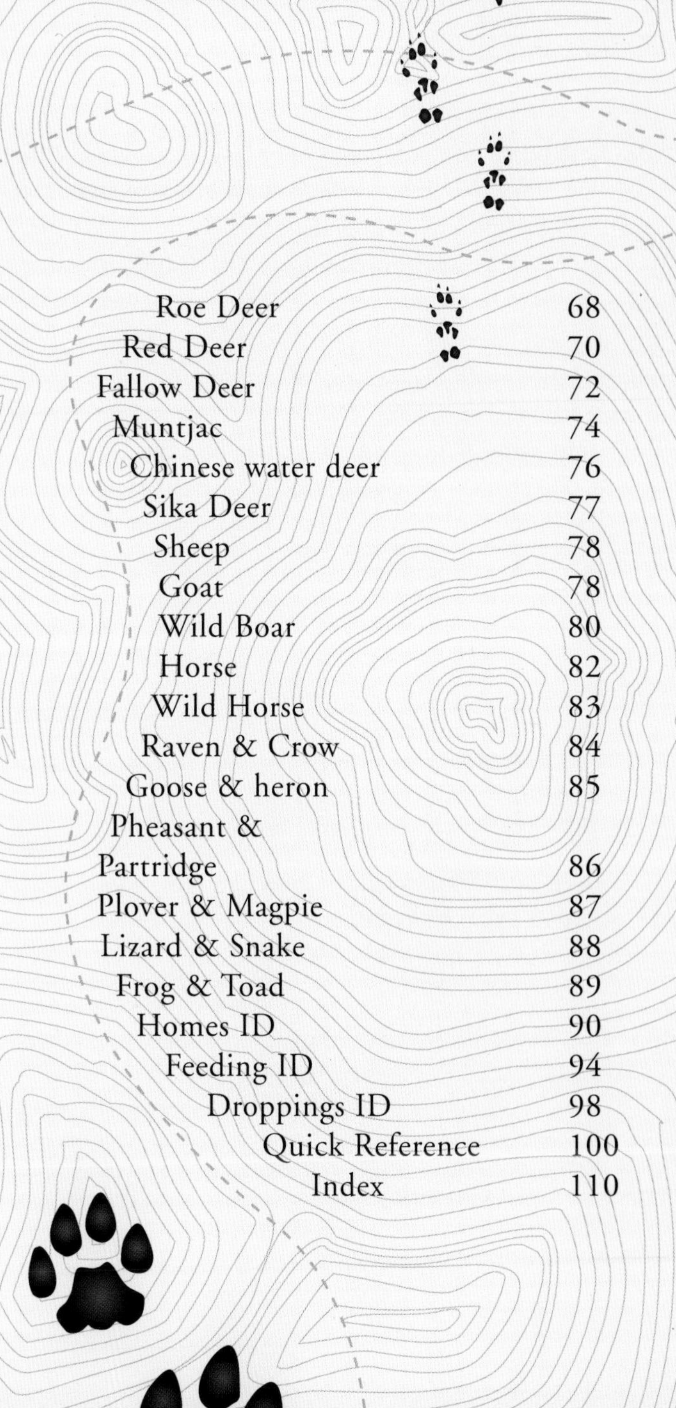

FOREWORD
by Ian Maxwell

On a patch of dry sand we found marks where large drops of water had fallen, almost certainly dewdrops knocked off the grass. This meant that the animals had been there after the dew had formed, probably between midnight and sun up. The footprints were dry and surrounded by the drops of water. The drops of water hadn't dried up and the tracks had clear sharp edges; this meant we were not far behind. Before long we came on the raiders' spoor in some trampled vegetation. There is always something exciting about coming on fresh spoor, no matter how much you have tracked. The sight of those great imprints make the jaw muscles tighten and chills run up your legs. The prospect of action lies ahead and that is always thrilling.

Everything leaves something of itself behind, and often that is footprints or spoor, long after an animal or human has passed, its footprints leave behind a story. The story can be read like a Sherlock Holmes or Agatha Christie novel. It will read of emotion, struggle and hardship. It will read of, Can I eat it? Can it eat me? Above all of survival.

I believe that within every man, woman and child there lurks a tracker. Indeed a primeval passion burns like a hot coal within some people. Tracking links us to the ancients who had to track to find food and track to defend. There is no greater and more timeless tool than the art of tracking, used to defend, to attack and most important of all, to feed hungry mouths.

Entering the woods and bush not knowing how to track is like entering a library and not knowing how to read a book. Both contain a wealth of information and just like a library, where every book tells a story, so does every track. There is a beginning, middle and an end, only that in tracking when you pick up one end of the string, at the other end is the animal.

Following tracks can be very exciting, however the most exciting of all is reading the tracks, who was the animal, not just the species, but which one. What was it doing at the time, why was it doing the action, where was it happening, and when did it happen.

Whilst tracking leopard early one morning in Africa it was very clear. Firstly the leopard print is distinct from other large cats in that its prints are slightly smaller. I had been tracking this leopard for several days and could recognise its prints from other leopards by a scar from a previous injury on its right hind pad. Whilst tracking I could tell it was on its way back to its lair after an unsuccessful nights hunting, I could tell this by the way that it was changing its direction of travel frequently. A hunting animal on its way to feed walks in a very business-like manner and will follow many scents to find its prey, sometimes zigzagging in and out of the scent cone of its prey. Once its has fed it will sit or lie down, maybe play, perhaps preen itself and wander on its way.

On this occasion it was following a dusty road, which was easier than going through the bush, and then suddenly it changed direction and headed into the bush. On following the tracks for a few meters I could see fresh tracks of a partridge going to a nest and none going out. There was dew on the grass around the tracks, and yet none inside the tracks, so I knew the leopard had changed direction to find the partridge after the dew came down which is likely to have come down about 3.00am, the edges of the tracks were sharp so I knew I was only an hour behind the leopard. This track came to an end at 2pm the same day. I tracked the leopard through the day whilst it was resting and finally came across it hiding in a thicket, it was nearly impossible to find. If wasn't for tracks I would never have found it.

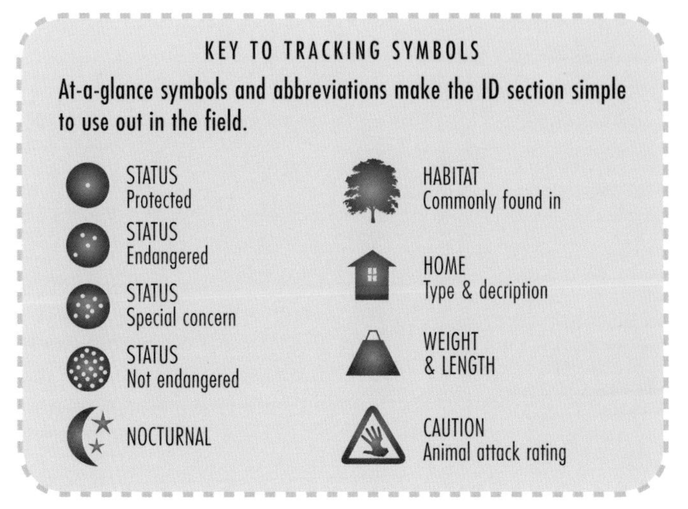

FOREWORD
by Ian Maxwell

Over the years that I have been tracking it is fair to say that it has been shrouded in mystery and exageration and in the last few years since I have been teaching tracking to wildlife enthusiasts, law enforcement agencies, forensic professionals and it is becoming more mainstream. Tracking is now far more accepted as a leisure pursuit and growing rapidly.

In 2006 I received a medal from Her Majesty The Queen at Buckingham Palace for "Tracking and Conservation of Large Cats" To my surprise I had a long talk with the Queen and found that she to was fascinated by tracking.

TV has helped to access the masses and with the broadcast of my TV program *"Big Cat Track"* on Animal Planet it will again convert many more to tracking. Part of the success of *"Big Cat Track"* was down to the excellent director, Nigel Janes, who was more used to directing fashion shows than tracking. He was able to bring to life the pleasures of tracking to thousands of viewers around the globe.

Several times a year I give talks to the public and after every talk people from all walks of life queue up to tell me that they have felt a deep desire to track but didn't know how to develop it. I run tracking courses around the world and am inspired by my instructors, some of whom struggled against the many enemies of tracking. They overcame the conscious and logical mind, they overcame ego, they tracked in some of the worst conditions I have ever known, they have persevered and have found tracks only given away by a single grain of white sand. Yet, they will come back time after time to every course to pass on their hard earned knowledge.

Children and youth feel thirst for the knowledge. My daughter Caitlin and my son Joshi are always up to some form of tracking and honing their skills. They are never happier than playing with sticks and tracking animals. On one occasion when Caitlin was five I picked her up from school only to find that she had gathered a large audience and was teaching them to stalk.

I had the honour of tracking with The Shadowwolves, a Native American tracking unit of The United States Department of Homeland Security deployed in Arizona. On leaving the unit I received one of their greatest honours and a simple letter from the supervisor "Make good use of your knowledge".

This book has been many years in the coming; at first I wasn't sure of the content or style. I didn't want it to be technical, but I wanted it to useful. I wanted it to include all the animals that I had tracked. I wanted it to be inspirational and contemporary and to that I am indebted to Joanna, the illustrator and designer for coming up with a fresh and easy to read design.

Never in my wildest of dreams and quietest of moments, in the deserts, forests and jungles of the world, did I ever imagine that tracking would take me to Buckingham Palace to meet the Queen, Lords, Ladies and honourable members of the House of Lords.

I have given many TV interviews around the world and on every occasion have shown them how the dry dust, blown by the wind tells its own story and leaves behind its own track. Every tracker should know the seasons and any variations on that should be noticed. I have noticed the landscape changing dramatically in most countries I have tracked in. It has been taken to have political meaning because of global warming and climate change.

I always wondered what would happen to the art of tracking. Yet as fate played its hand, childhood games to rhino wars I find myself at a stage in life where it has become my dream to pass on my knowledge through this book *"Animal Tracks ID and Techniques"*.

It is a tribute to all those whom have I have tracked with. The free and pioneering spirit of my parents. The courage of my great father, the compassion and energy of my dear mother and the raw energy of my son Joshi and my daughter Caitlin who are already trackers that I am very proud of.

The author entices a fox to come closer by rustling a feather.

HOW TO USE THIS BOOK

The tracks in this book are derived from British and European wildlife. Some of the tracks include exotic animals that are roaming the UK and Europe.

- Photographs accompany most species.
- The print pattern is contained in an easy to read window and include the scale of the diagram to the real track.
- The track window includes rear and front tracks for most of the animals.
- 1:1 Equals the actual track size of an adult animal
- 1:2 You should double the size of the diagram to match an actual track
- Gait Pattern is the moving pattern of the animal. This can be influenced by landscape and speed of movement.
- Diagonal Walkers means that they move opposite sides of the body, at the same time ,moving the right front foot at the same time as the rear left foot.
- Bounders means that when the animal pushes off with its back feet they land just behind the front feet, which have landed a very short period before. These tracks are usually in groups of four.
- Galloper. All four legs propel the animal forward. The front may land side by side with the rear feet, then the rear feet are brought ahead of the front feet.
- Direct Registration means that the animal places the back track inside the track of the front track.
- Indirect registration means that the animal normally places its back track partly on the front track.
- Compression Shape. The shaded area indicates the over-all shape of the track which may be the only thing visible on grass, pine needles ,sand or hard surfaces.

GUIDE TO ICONS

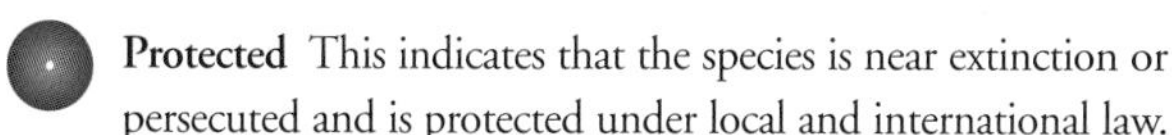

Protected This indicates that the species is near extinction or persecuted and is protected under local and international law.

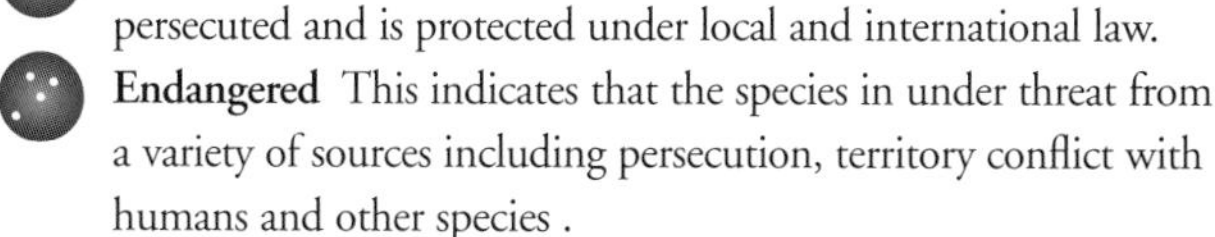

Endangered This indicates that the species in under threat from a variety of sources including persecution, territory conflict with humans and other species .

Special Concern Shows viability of the species within an area, subject to various factors including persecution, territory conflict and dominant species pressure. The species identified with this icon are not endangered but deserve special concern

Not Endangered This species is viable and successful in its given environment

Habitat Indicates the likely location of a species. All animals can vary significantly in their chosen environment ,dependent on ecological niches. The habitat is a generalisation and by no means exhaustive.

Home Describes the type of home a species will inhabit. Animals are opportunists and may vary from the description dependant on location and competition for homes. This is a generalisation and not exhaustive

Weight and length This gives an average adult species weight and length. Animals can vary significantly from location to location dependant on competition for food and environment. Young species and sub-adult animals are not included.

Caution This indicates the attack and danger rating of an animal. It applies to animals that are very obviously dangerous. All animals can be dangerous and even small animals can inflict serious bites. This icon does not cover diseases that an animal can cause. Some animals can pass on on dangerous diseases and you should be cautious of this at all times

Nocturnal Indicates that the animal may be active at night

HOW TO TRACK

When learning to track it is important to read and understand the landscape. By doing this and plotting yourself into the landscape, you will be creating a virtual bird's eye view of barriers and features that would attract an animal, including time of day, shadows and vegetation.

- There are three types of barrier. Natural barriers, rivers, lakes, mountains. Manmade barriers, roads, fences, walls and dams. In addition to these barriers there is also the food barrier that prevents movement away from the food source.
- The best way to find spoor is to cast around, looking along the ground towards the sun and also look up for aerial spoor confirming each other as you go.
- There are some skills that are worth practicing, that will deliver better results. Don't be discouraged if at first you have difficulty finding spoor, it will come with practice and knowing where to look and what to look for.
- A stick is a good aid to tracking, it helps to focus where the tracks might be and helps to point them out ahead.

AWARENESS

The most important skill any tracker can have is awareness. I have been teaching this using the Phase Technique. I called it the Phase Technique, because, rather like a light bulb being turned up using a dimmer, so can the trackers awareness be turned up. The bulb must pass through stages before it receives its full energy and burns brightest. Just like the light bulb we need to practice some skills that will bring you closer to nature, animals and your state of total sensory awareness.

One Sense It has often been said that we have five senses; some people say that we have six senses. I have found that where all the five senses are working as one the tracker has only one sense, all the physical senses are combined creating someone who is highly tuned in, and this is what is believed to be the sixth sense, though in reality it is the combination of all the senses. When referring to the physical senses, it is very important that they represent something to us.

On one course I used a cloth covered in scented perfume for the trackers to follow, using their nose. At the de-briefing one of the girls said that when she could smell the perfume that she saw her grandmother in her mind. So it is with any sense. When you hear the sea, you should envision the sea. When you smell an apple, you should see the apple. When you touch the ground at night with your toes, you should envision the surface. When you taste a strawberry you should feel it, and smell it. When you see an object you should envision what it would feel like, what it may sound like, what it may smell like and maybe also, what it would taste like. In short every sense must have a meaning to a tracker, not just that he could smell fresh dug soil, but that they should enquire as to what the digging did.

Feeling This refers to the touching of another object; we normally associate this with fingers. However we can feel many things with other part of the body. We can feel the wind with the tongue. Or we could feel rough bark of a tree or the moisture in the air with our skin.
Seeing This refers to using sight, but is not only restricted to the eyes. The brain can play tricks on the eyes, and it is possible that the eyes are not actually seeing the object physically. The tracker must be able to see objects, even with their eyes closed.
Listening This is referred to as hearing, however listening is different to hearing. To a tracker the bark of a deer will mean many things. The alarm calls of birds will tell a tracker of the presence of a predator and indeed the size and direction of the predator.
Taste Sometimes taste and smell can be together. As a child, I was balanced on a wall eating mulberries. I was gorging away, when suddenly, I felt a sharp taste and smell at the same time. I had bitten through a stink-bug, a beetle which defences are to create a strong smell to predators. I will never forget the sensation and can only describe as feeling like getting a broken nose. When I smell anything similar, to this day I envision the bug.
Smell As mentioned above the sensation of smell and taste are connected. I often get strange looks when I ask to people smell tap or clear river water. Because it is clear they assume it will have no smell. Try it; you will be amazed by the variation in the smell of water.

Now let's combine all the senses, and you will be amazed.

HOW TO TRACK

I have been tracking at night with no lights for many years. It was a technique that was shrouded with exaggeration. The media made it look as though the Cheyenne, Apaches and Zulus Impis were the only people to be able to this. During a course I asked a class to attempt it. At first I was met with disbelief. Within a few hours, they were on their hands and knees in pitch black, smelling the tracks, feeling the tracks and seeing the tracks. As I watched twelve trackers through night vision binoculars I was amazed to see that all of them were accurately following the tracks, footprint by footprint.

ZONING IN

The Zone In is the anvil for the tracker. To do this you must find a spot where you can sit and clear the mind of troubles and plot yourself into the landscape. The tracker must be like a mirror and reflect what is around them. At first you might be concerned by mosquitoes, midges or other insects. You might be worried that it will rain or be too hot or too cold. You will have to surrender to all around you. Once you surrender and become part of your surroundings you will have zoned in. You will now be able to hear every movement, every sound, see everything and feel everything around you.

I have experienced many more close encounters with wildlife after zoning in than at any other time.

Recently I had just finished zoning in, when a nearby herd of elephants made an unexpected turn directly towards me. I was in a difficult position because I had been sitting on a solitary fallen fever tree which was surrounded by open ground. If I had run or walked away they would have certainly charged because they had several calves. I stayed on my tree, knowing that the tree was a favourite for passing elephants to rub against. The large matriarch acknowledged me with a violent shake of the ears as they passed silently by within two meters.

BASELINE

Once you have zoned in for at least twenty minutes you will know the baseline for noises, bird song, activity, motion and insect life. You will also know the baseline for the ground, trees and shrubs in the landscape around you.

It is here that the tracker will detect any variation from the baseline, be it hearing, feeling, seeing, smelling and taste.

We will look to ground for ground spoor and above ankle height for aerial spoor. Information gathering can save a lot of time, so speak to the gamekeeper, local naturalist and wildlife enthusiasts, and of course the internet can provide lots of useful information.

Because animals are mostly creatures of habit, they will use the same trails and runs between sleeping places, water and food source. Invariably these are likely to be the most direct routes available.. These 'roadways' are excellent places to find tracks.

HOW TO TRACK

WHAT TO LOOK FOR IN THE LANDSCAPE

You should be thinking back to your zone-in and plotted yourself into the landscape. What will influence the animal you are tracking? What are the physical features around you? Look for ponds, lakes and rivers where wildlife will drink. Trails will lead to and from water via the easiest route. There are also changeable factors like shadow. Although shadow is not part of the landscape, it is caused by the landscape and the sun. Whilst tracking for the Brazilian wildlife department I used shadows to track puma. At the time they were getting lots of livestock predation and wanted to know if the puma was living in the jungle and travelling out to hunt. In vain they put camera traps around the reserve in the hope that they would get a photograph of the culprit and had no success in a year. After a couple of days I was called to a sheep kill, and from there using the time of day and where the shadow was cast by a bank just before the kill was made I was able to track a puma mother and cub into the reserve.

In these areas look for soft mud where you will find excellent track traps. Animals always travel along the path of least resistance unless they are in pursuit of food or evading a predator.

The best places to see tracks in the wild are along dirt roads, or tracks. Often tracks can be found along well worn game paths which will lead to and from water.

These trails are used by most animals, it is not specialised and like a manifold will have lots of smaller runs leading into it.

Along the trails look for track traps. These are areas of dry sand, or soft mud, where animals have to pass through.

If the animal has been funnelled into the track traps you are in a prime spot. I often check farm gates, where the mud is softened by sheep or cattle. In the soft areas I almost always find fox or badger tracks, and one occasion in England found puma tracks.

WHERE TO LOOK

There is an African saying, "There is no point looking for deer in the ocean". I use this all the time when forming a mental picture of what I am tracking. Recently whilst looking for the Iberian Lynx, the world's most endangered cat, I learned that its staple diet consists almost exclusively of rabbits and partridge. In the Algarve region of Portugal, rabbit is very scarce. It was a simple equation. First look for rabbits and the lynx should be nearby. Within three days I had found a lynx, the first one in that area for many years. In many ways, animals are just like instruments whose 'tune' is 'played' by the landscape.

To be a tracker, you have to think like a the animal you are tracking, the tracker must have empathy with whatever they are following. Use all your powers of observation and, just as importantly, learn to make the connections between what your senses tell you. Assess the landscape you're tracking in. Make notes. What water and vegetation is available? What are the sources of food? Where are the paths of least resistance, the barriers both natural and manmade?

Food source has the biggest influence. I was working with Brazilian and Argentine anti-poaching rangers in an area where the poachers were shooting capybaras, tapir and wild pigs in the jungle. To make their lives easier, the poachers put salt onto the branches of trees. Herbivores are attracted by salt and soon become addicted to it. Once they are addicted they start gathering in large concentrations around the salt licks. Jaguars are attracted to the area because of the abundance of food. In a similar fashion otters do the same and gather close to fish farms where there is lots of food. The same can be said of any animal, find their food and water source and not too far away you will find the animal.

Always look in track traps, along trails and runs. By knowing the animal you are tracking you will know where to look for tracks. I have tracked many otters and by knowing where they are likely to occur, it is never very long before I turn up fresh otter tracks. They like running water, hopefully a bridge for cover, a good food source and that's where you will find them.

Recently in Dorset, I saw some otter spraint under a bridge, I continued tracking and within a few minutes an otter made a star appearance, rolled on its back and swam off.

Once you have found your tracks it will become a lot easier when you are able to anticipate where the next print will be and what it the compression shape would look like if it is not perfectly formed in the mud or sand.

HOW TO TRACK

WHAT TO LOOK FOR ON THE GROUND: GROUND SPOOR

On the ground look for flattening of sand, mud or broken twigs and fallen leaves that have been stood on. If an animal with paws has stood on something it is harder to track than something with hooves. Soft paws will spread, where-as a hoof will push a stone or twig into the ground. Although soft paws will give, if the animal has claws you maye be able to see claw marks in the ground.

Look for bruised vegetation, feathers and dens. Usually the easiest spoor on the ground to see is the primary impact point of the foot. The PIP is where the foot strikes the ground first, the hind pad, heel of a human or the rear part of a deer hoof.

Colour change Look for changes in colour. Upturned leaves on trees are usually light green on the underside and dark green on the top. A stone recently kicked out of its socket will leave the socket dark (because of moisture content) until it dries out. Look for animal hairs on gates and brambles. A freshly gnawed nut will be lighter the more recent it is. Fresh tracks in a wet landscape will look lighter than the surrounding, because they have pushed water out. Fresh tracks on sandy ground in a hot climate will look darker because of the moisture content underneath the surface being exposed.

Context Look for anything out of baseline or context. Discolouration or disturbance.

When tracking in pine needles the only thing you may see is the random pattern of the needles being slightly disturbed and forming a compression shape of the animals paw or hoof. Look for pushed-up leaves and soil that wild boar or badger have disturbed whilst looking for food.

It is also very useful to study animal scat and insect activity on the ground. I have found that if something has recently been disturbed then the insects act in a random pattern in an attempt to escape and find cover. This can be seen disrupted ant trails, and wood lice, where bark has been knocked off from decaying wood.

Spider webs can be studied to establish if a den in the ground is currently being used an animal.

WHAT TO LOOK FOR OFF THE GROUND: AERIAL SPOOR

When I am tracking and cannot find prints on the ground, I will look at plants for feeding signs. Recently in an area where I run tracking courses there was a lot of forestry work being carried out and I noticed that I was seeing fewer deer than the year before. Their tracks were not on the road. However they had been feeding on fresh shoots about one meter off the ground and from the side of the road. Because of the activity of the machines they had become very shy and had learned to feed whilst in cover. I could tell where they were standing by the angle of the cut on the shoots. On looking closer the deer had started a new trail, behind the thick vegetation at the side of the road.

Trees and vegetation These can show areas where animals have been gnawing or rubbing against.

Animal feeding signs Look for animal feeding signs, deer that have gnawed at fresh bramble shoots, wild boar that have pushed up the ground looking for tasty roots.

Badgers that have been scratching trees looking for grubs. Animal remains can tell you a lot about its primary cause of death and what has been feeding on it. Often I find that an animal may have been killed by an ambush predator, and that by the time I come across it the remains are dominated by scavenger spoor. This can happen overnight. I have seen animals killed by ambush predators and by the morning the carcass has been dispersed by badger, fox, crows and even seagulls.

It is also useful to watch what ground feeding birds are doing. If they are popping up from the trees into mid-air then there is a very dangerous predator nearby. If they are hooking up into a tree or bush, there is a predator nearby. The height that they go to indicates the size of the predator, by the height at which it could leap.

Spider webs are good aerial spoor and often they not entirely broken by something passing through. The size of the animal passing through will influence the height at which the web-strands are broken.

HOW TO TRACK

WHAT TO LISTEN TO

The language of birds is one of the most useful tricks that a tracker can have. It does not have to be vocal nor is it specialised to any specific bird. Generally the language of any ground feeding bird will be able to give us lots of clues. They will tell us if there is a predator nearby that they know, or is a stranger to the area, how big the predator is and the threat level of the predator.

Birds will call if they see a predator; this alarm will be picked up by other birds and animals and repeated. Insects will also alarm when a predator is detected. Alarm signalling birds will tip-off the deer that there is a threat, the deer will in turn alert other deer, bark and run. The threat level will be vocalised by the intensity of the alarm call. For example, a weasel will cause an intense alarm call, as opposed to a fat cat aimlessly wondering around a garden.

Nature hates silence, and just as birds and insects may alarm, they will also go silent if a predator gets too close. This is very common where a bird of prey is active and flying through the territory.

AGE OF SPOOR

The assessment of the numerous factors which may indicate the age of spoor is one of the most difficult aspects of tracking.

- As soon as spoor is made the effects of the elements and gravity set to work.
- The effect of the sun, wind, rain , and other factors will cause the tracks to age.
- Aging can be done by direct questioning, experience or comparison.
- Vegetation can be aged by studying vegetation In the area you are tracking. It should be possible to tell if the damage took place within a few minutes, hours or days.
- Recent injuries to plants will show weeping at the wound site, after several hours this will dry up, after several days it will become dark.
- I often use rain to age tracks. By keeping a record of rain-fall, I will know when the track was made, based on the condition of the track floor. If the track was made after it rained there will be an absence of rain marks in the track floor, and if it was before it will contain rain marks.
- The definition and sharpness of the edge of the track will also show the age. The sharper the edge, the more recent. If part of the track has fallen into the track floor, the older it is.

There are many factors to indicate the age, including spider webs, dew and insect activity to age tracks. Scat can also be aged. In the first few hours it will attract flies and other insects. It is very common for beetles to gather scat for feeding on. After a few hours the scat will develop a crust and after that the insect activity will diminish.

Generally I age spoor into four categories.
Very fresh Within minutes or seconds
Fresh Within two hours, fours hours or eight hours.
Medium After eight hours but within 24 hours
Old After 24 hours, 48 hours, one week, or two weeks.

ACTIVE OR PASSIVE TRACKS

Tracking is like picking up a piece of string and at the other end there should be an animal. Animals move freely within their home range and will know every rock, tunnel, bush and tree. Within that area they feel safe and you will find lots of tracks.

Outside the home range the animal will be very aware of its surroundings. This will be reflected by the direction of tracks and whether the tracks show any signs of stopping and the type of stops. Usually a sudden stop means that the animal is out of its home range. This coupled with the fact that its tracks may be erratic and hopefully fresh are tracks that are active and worth following.
Active Fresh tracks going in one direction.
Passive Old tracks that have been stood on by the animal since they were made.

HOW TO TRACK

LIGHT

We need to utilise sunlight and the angle at which it illuminates the tracks. Low angles are best, and therefore I find tracking early in the morning or late afternoon is the best time. Tracking mid winter on a sunny day is the best you can get.

The worst time to track is when the sun is at its highest. Tracking when the sun is at its highest can be overcome by using a wide brimmed hat and mirror. Cover the track with a good shadow. Then using a mirror reflect sunlight over the track from a low angle. You will be amazed by the detail you can see. It is essential that you keep the track between you and the sun and vary your height. If you are tracking at night keep the tracks between you and the torch.

LOST SPOOR

Losing spoor is very easy to do. This can also indicate that the tracker is tired or "tracked out". Tracking is very intense and hard work on the brain and eyes.

I find that once people become tracked out, they become frustrated because they are no longer seeing tracks. All that needs to be done is to take a rest and within a few minutes the tracks will start to appear again. It is recommended that you track in pairs. The tracker is always looking at the ground whilst the other person is looking ahead for sightings or danger.

The angle of the sun may change or a cloud may come over. I have seen obvious tracks, looked up for a couple of seconds and they have disappeared.

While you are tracking, mark spoor every ten to twenty meters with your stick. If you lose the spoor, mark the last known track and move back, taking care not to stand on any tracks. Look around and to your left and right, then in the most likely direction of travel. If you are still unable to find the spoor, cast around in a ever-increasing circle. By doing this you should be able to pick the tracks up again.

GETTING CLOSE

So now you are getting close, you will have to move silently and be down wind. By moving slowly you become less visible to animals.

The most important factor when getting close is to move silently and pick your route from cover to cover. This may not be the most direct route and can take several hours.

I have stalked into the middle of a troop of hundreds of baboons and a herd of Cape Buffalo, by moving from cover to cover and when the wind is favourable. Once you are inside a herd then collective behaviour will cause them to not feel threatened. It is the approach to animals that is crucial. If they see, smell or hear you they will run off.

If the wind is blowing then it must be in your face, so that you are down-wind of the animal. A useful way of estimating the direction of the wind is to run some dust or light dirt through your fingers. The dust will travel in the same direction as the wind

After you have chosen your route take care so that when you place your feet that you don't crack a twig or cause leaves to rustle.

Raise one foot at a time and bring it slowly down on the entire outside of the foot, rolling it in-wards in a flowing motion, so that you can feel what you are stepping on.

It is important that the foot is placed on the ground before weight of the body is committed. That way if you feel a twig you can re-position your foot. It may be that you will have to crawl to get closer.

Whilst tracking some animals you can get closer by moving when their head is down feeding. As soon as they raise their head, then you must freeze until their head is down again. As long as you are down wind and moving silently you will be surprised just how close you can get.

HOW TO TRACK

Casting tracks is good fun. I have seen some impressive collections of tracks. One friend travels the world to track animals and cast their prints. She has literally got hundreds including badger, bear, kangaroo and lion.

YOU WILL NEED

- Plaster of paris
- Water
- Paper clip
- Plastic pot
- Cardboard or plastic strip

- Once you have found a good track, make a cardboard or plastic rim around it, about 30mm depth. Tape or clip the ends together then press the rim into the ground.
- Mix the plaster according to the manufacturers recommendations. Ensuring the mixing container is free from old plaster debris. Mix only enough plaster for the print you are casting.
- Usually around 2 parts of plaster to one of water is used. The consistency should resemble pancake mix.
- Pour the plaster slowly and carefully into the mould.
- Pour first into areas of high detail, then pour the plaster to cover the track evenly. The thicker the cast the better. It may also be an idea to re-enforce the cast by adding debris or spare paper clips. Plaster of paris is soft and if a large print is cast, it is advisable to re-enforce it.
- Leave the cast to set for as long as possible. When the plaster is dry it will appear matt and be hard to touch.
- Pick the cast up by sliding your hand underneath and lifting. Do not pry with a sharp object as this is likely to damage the plaster.
- Take the cast home and put it in a warm dry place before cleaning. Painting the animal detail of the cast will make it look good, especially if you use hobby battleship grey and blue.
- Dental stone can be used instead of plaster.

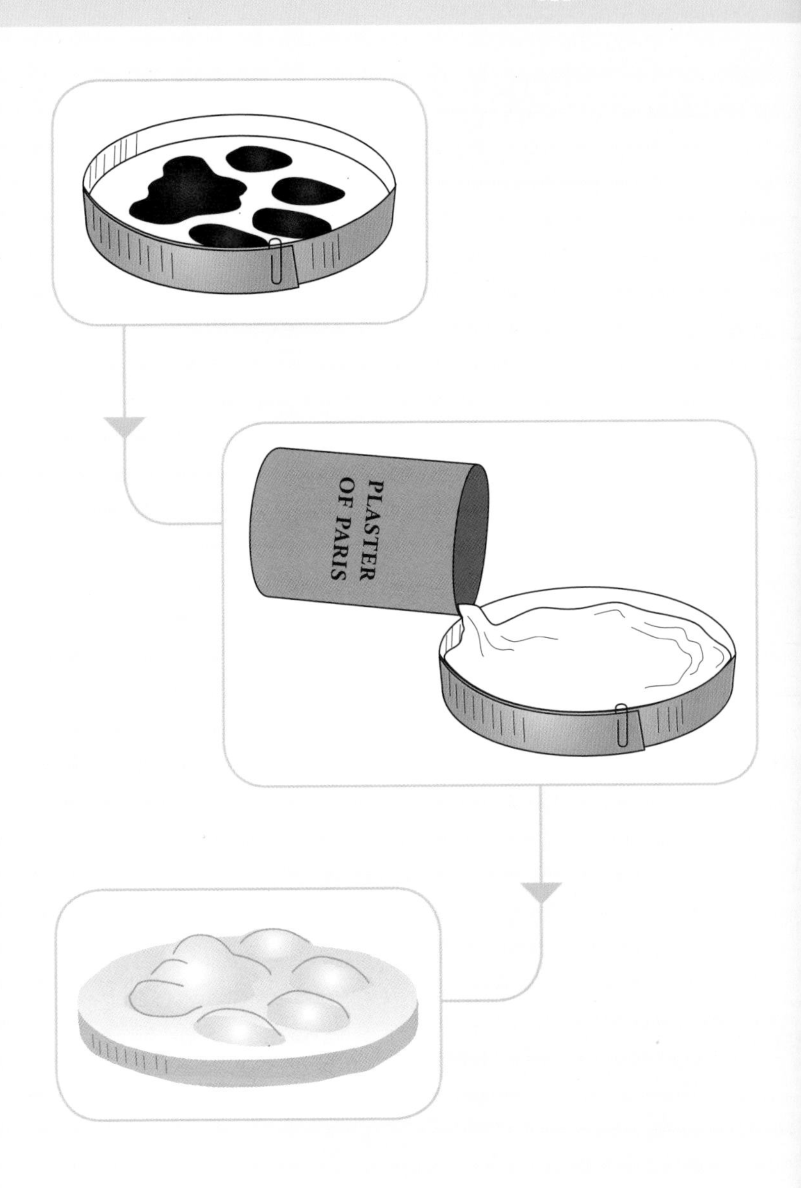
PLASTER
OF PARIS

The fox is found throughout Europe and Britain. It is very common in towns and cities where it has lost its fear of humans and now lives in harmony. It is dog-like in appearance with light underparts, chin and throat, it can also appear very dark and almost black.

They especially favour the edges of woods and fields. Tracks can usually be found along bridle ways, paths and trails.

A fox will eat most things including berries, fruit, grass, small mammals and birds. Fox tracks are usually smaller and slender than that of a dog with the two front pads a long way in front of other pads. Fox scat is easily spotted where it will mark its territory in very conspicuous spots, including rocks.

3- 7kgs
55-65cms

SCALE
1:1
GAIT PATTERN
Diagonal/Indirect
COMPRESSION SHAPE
Oval

GRAY WOLF
(Canis lupus)

The Gray Wolf is also known as the Timberwolf. They have been exterminated in many parts of the world because of their predation on livestock. Wolves are surrounded by superstition and humans have a curious fear of the wolf. The wolf used to range throughout the United States, and as a result of their feeding on livestock were exterminated as part of a government program.

Wolves are carnivorous predators, scavengers and, strangely enough, they are herbivores, eating plants for vitamins and minerals. They may also eat livestock and garbage. They use complex vocal communications, including specialised howls between each other when hunting, and will call others when a source of food and prey is located.

Usually they will hunt in packs, attacking large prey such as deer, caribou, moose, oxen and bison, biting at the rump, shoulder and flank until the animal collapses. They prefer to attack the old, sick and young animals. They will also eat sheep, goats, cows and smaller prey such as rabbits and rodents (including beavers). They can eat as much as 10kgs of food in one meal, however if they can't eat it all, they may cover the partially eaten carcass with dirt and vegetation only to return later to finish the meal.

TRACKER'S TALE

Ask a person what they think about a wolf before they see the tracks, and they will usually reply 'Big Teeth'. Ask them after they've seen their first footprints, and they will usually say 'Big feet'. When I saw my first fresh wolf prints in Canada, I couldn't sleep. It was so good to know that they were nearby.

Because they usually eat all of the carcass, the scat will have hair and bones visible, and may include seeds and grass. Wolves will mark their territory with urine, and leave droppings in the middle of a trail to advertise their presence in the area. Conservation efforts are in progress around the world to re-introduce and re-populate areas where they have become extinct. Conservation programs in Scotland are looking at re-population of the wolf where it has been extinct since the 1700s. Wolf tracks are spectacular with exaggerated toe pads, and long, pronounced claw marks.

30-50kg
1-1.7m

TRACKER'S TIP
Wolves are the wild ancestors of dogs. They have a reflective retina in their eyes that enhances night vision. A pack consists of a dominant alpha male who is pack leader, and an omega wolf at the bottom who bears the brunt of re-directed aggression from the rest of the pack.

DOMESTIC DOG

(Canis)

Not endangered

Den

Widespread

Dog prints are the most common tracks found near to civilisation and because they are related to fox and wolves the prints have similar characteristics. They can also resemble large cat prints.

The difference between dog and wolf and fox is that the track line for fox and wolf is usually straight whereas the dog will normally zig-zag. The difference between large cats and dog prints are that claw marks are visible on a dog and usually absent in cats. The front two toes of dog prints are usually in line and the heel pad has two lobes on the back. A cat will have three lobes. The compression shape of a dog is oval and a cat is round.

Variable weight and size

TRACKER'S TIP
Dog prints come in a large variation of shapes. Remember the tip which refers to the shape of the print:" If its round it aint a hound"

LYNX
(Felis lynx)

Endangered

Trees and holes

Dense forest

Nocturnal

The European lynx is also known as the Northern or Eurasian lynx. It is typically found in northern forest and Steppe across Europe and Asia. It has a stocky body with long powerful legs, a short black-tipped tail and prominent tufted ears.

The dense fur varies in coloration but is the upper part of the coat is normally a yellowish brown with darker spots and the lower part is lighter in colour. The European lynx have more spots than the American species The tracks of a lynx are disproportionately large to the animal and have lots of fur between the digits.

It also has a neck-ruff with black and white markings which fans open as an aggressive visual signal. The harsh environments these animals typically habitat mean they have a very broad diet, from small deer to rats, mice and lemmings, but normally they prey on rabbits and hares.

They give birth to between 1-4 young that begin to accompany their mother at about 3 months old. Mated pairs or a mother and young sometimes hunt together. The Eurasian Lynx has been intensively hunted and trapped for its valuable fur, and because it is considered a threat to game and livestock. It is a CITES listed species and re-introductions have recently taken place in parts of Germany, Austria, Switzerland and Slovenia.

7-15kg
70-90cm

SCALE
1:1.5
GAIT PATTERN
Diagonal/Direct
COMPRESSION SHAPE
Round

PUMA
(Felis concolor)

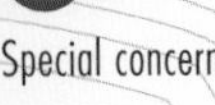

Special concern

Rocky areas

Mountains and forest

Nocturnal

Sometimes called a cougar or mountain lion originates from South America, Mexico and North America. The coat is sandy brown and they have a muscular frame. It is believed that these were kept as designer pets in Europe and as the result of release and escape they roam freely throughout the UK and Europe.

It is a secretive and nocturnal creature and so sighting are very rare. The tracks rarely show claw marks except in soft mud or snow and when used for traction.

Other spoor to watch out for is scratching on trees, covering of droppings and concealed kills where the puma will return to later.

TRACKER'S TALE

I have tracked puma in Brazil and whilst they are very secretive they are creatures of habit and I found their tracks easy to locate. I was called to a farm in Brazil where puma had killed some sheep and the behaviour was to bite at the base of the skull and drag the kill into cover. I have observed the same behaviour in the many sheep kills I have attended in the UK.

50-110kg
2-2.5m

TRACKER'S TIP
Scratch markings on trees can often indicate the direction of travel. Find the shadows and you will find the puma.

LEOPARD
(Panthera pardus)

Protected

Rocky areas

Remote savanna & forest

Nocturnal

Leopards are shy, solitary, cunning, fierce and are more stealthy than any other feline. They are expert climbers and can be found in a wide range of habitats. They are extremely dangerous when cornered or disturbed. They are usually golden yellow with distinct black spots.

Some leopards have been bred to be black and are called melanistic leopards where the spots have joined up. Like other large cats these were designer pets and have been released or escaped and believed to be roaming the United Kingdom.

They usually kill their prey by biting through the throat or nape of the neck and will sometimes drag their prey up into a tree to keep the food away from other scavengers. The leopard is a highly evolved and expert ambush predator. Surprisingly leopard are found very close to human habitation. In some areas of the world they have developed a taste for dogs

TRACKER'S TALE

I have tracked leopard in various parts of the world and have always found them very difficult to spot. I use a trick of looking through undergrowth or leaves to spot them and usually find that it is their eyes that give their position away. They always look very aggressive when spotted and a good friend of mine lost his fingers to a leopard he surprised. Leopard was the first animal I tracked as a child.

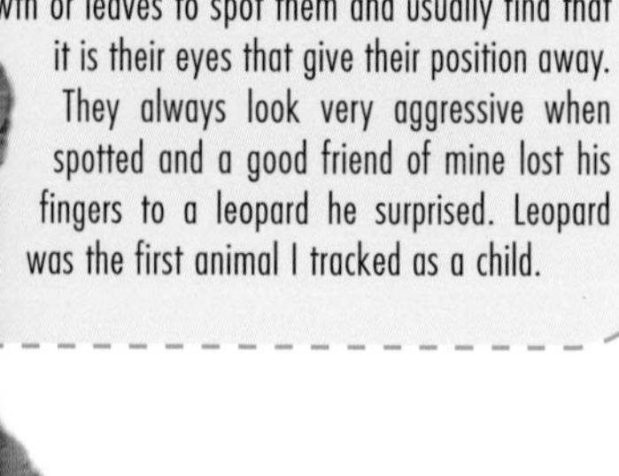

30-90kg
1.5-2m

TRACKER'S TIP
Find the shadows and you will find the leopard.

CARACAL
(Felis caracal)

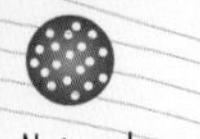

Not endangered

Small caves

Hilly country

Nocturnal

The Caracal originates in Africa and is sandy brown in colour with a short stocky tail and tufts on its ears. It is nocturnal and solitary and can be very fierce and will spit loudly.

It is believed that caracals may be roaming freely in the UK. The caracal hunts by knocking its prey down with a sideways blow and is able to snatch a flying bird from the air.

TRACKER'S TALE

I have been to a heron that was killed in the UK. The kill had all the characteristic traits of a caracal hunting. This was corroborated by the fact that there were large prints in the exact area that the heron was found.

SCALE
1:1.5
GAIT PATTERN
Diagonal/Direct
COMPRESSION SHAPE
Round

10-18kg
60-95cm

DOMESTIC CAT
(Felis catus)

Not endangered

Widespread

Nocturnal

Domestic cats come in all shapes and sizes, however their tracks are too small to be confused with other large cats and more rounded than those of a dog or fox. In addition there will be no claw marks. Domestic cats do not direct register with their paws, whereas as wild and feral cats place their back paws on top of the front print to minimise crunching of vegetation.

It is also easy to see stalking tracks and those that leap or bound. Domestic cats are excellent for watching to see how bird react to their presence in a hunting or relaxed mode.

TRACKER'S TALE

Watch how birds react to a stalking cat. They will appear to hook onto the nearest branch, just out of leaping distance and make alarm calls. As the cat moves along it will appear as though there was an inverted bowl of birds moving with the cat as they point out to others where the cat is located. If the cat gets too close it will go quiet.

SCALE
1:1
GAIT PATTERN
Diagonal/Indirect
COMPRESSION SHAPE
Round

2-7kg
70cm

BADGER
(Meles meles)

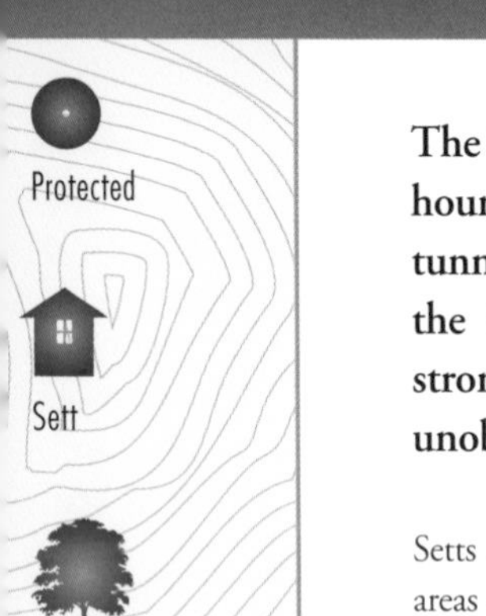

Forest

Nocturnal

The badger is nocturnal and spends the daylight hours in their social groups underground in tunnel systems known as setts. The badger is the fastest digging animal on earth, and the strongest for its size. They are common but very unobtrusive so can easily be overlooked.

Setts are almost invariably constructed in forests or other areas with woody cover, but foraging is mainly done in open areas such as fields.

Badgers have short legs and large bodies so their low bellies often brush along the ground when they clamber over roots and tufts of grass. A badger trail is recognizable by the crushed vegetation at ground level. Tracks show 5 toes and long claws with the fore foot being larger than the hind.

Badgers eat an extremely wide variety of foods. Insects, other invertebrates, small mammals and reptiles, fruits and other plant matter, and carrion are all part of their diet.

TRACKER'S TALE

I once followed some very old badger tracks from a sett and found a whole badger skeleton on the trail complete with skull. The badgers had created a new trail from the woods to the fields beyond which curved around the obstacle of their dead friend.

They leave a small depression in the ground while searching for plant bulbs. Another telltale sign that a badger has been feeding is that parts of the bulb may be found on the woodland floor. They use latrines usually found a small distance away from the sett. In the spring badger scat can contain large amounts of fur and bone from small rabbits eaten whilst in the burrow.

8-12kg
65-72cm

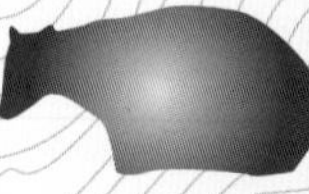

TRACKER'S TIP
A badger trail often has a distinctive earthy smell which is caused by secretions from anal glands.

OTTER
(Lutra lutra)

Protected

Holt

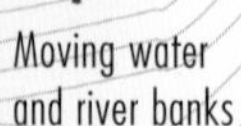

Moving water and river banks

Nocturnal

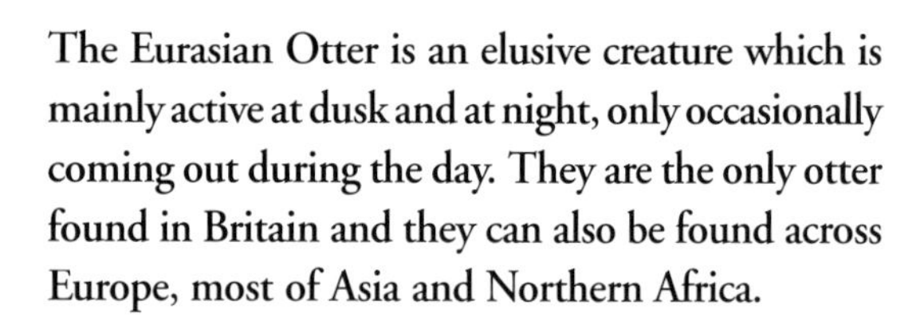

The Eurasian Otter is an elusive creature which is mainly active at dusk and at night, only occasionally coming out during the day. They are the only otter found in Britain and they can also be found across Europe, most of Asia and Northern Africa.

They feed on fish, frogs, crustaceans, voles and birds and have many adaptations to enable them to be efficient hunters in an aquatic environment. Otters have webbed feet with five toes and small claws and extremely dense insulation fur. They also have a thick, rudder-like tail for propulsion at speed through the water and they can close their nostrils and their ears when under the surface.

Otters are wonderfully playful animals and seem to take immense pleasure in sliding down muddy banks and throwing pebbles in the air. In fact when they are not hunting, they are more than likely having fun!

Otters are mostly solitary, except for when they are mating or with young. They dig a den called a holt which usually has an underwater entrance in the riverbank. They will return to the holt to sleep in the day but as they have such a large range they also form temporary rest sites in vegetation along the waterway called couches. They mark their territories by sprainting (defecating) in high places where the wind can carry the scent.

4-11kg
60-130cm

TRACKER'S TIP
Look under bridges for otter scat (spraint) that smells like jasmine tea!

STOAT
(Mustela erminea)

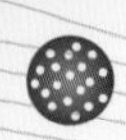

Not endangered

Trees and holes

Woodland and meadows

Nocturnal

Also known as the ermine or the short-tailed weasel. The stoat is an opportunistic carnivore which will eat rabbits, small mammals, birds, eggs, fish, reptiles and invertebrates. It is a very skilful tree climber and can descend a trunk headfirst, like a squirrel.

The stoat is capable of killing animals much larger than itself. They will often store extra food for later when it is plentiful.

The stoat's coat is mostly brown with an off-white belly. In winter, the coat is thicker and the colour changes to clean white when in northern areas with a lot of snow. It is during this white winter coat stage that they are referred to as ermine. In all seasons it has a black tip on its tail. Both males and females will cover large areas when hunting and they typically use several dens, often taken from prey species.

The stoat prefers to live in moorland, woods, farmland, marshes, sand dunes and hedgerows.

They are widespread throughout the British Isles and are also found throughout the rest of northern Europe, the tundra and temperate forest regions of Asia and North America.

A Stoat will often perform a peculiar dance as part of its hunting strategy. It will approach a group of birds or rabbits and then jump around, pretending to ignore the animals who are attracted to this bizarre behaviour and edge nearer to get a better look! The stoat then suddenly pounces on the nearest member of its audience!

SCALE
1:1
GAIT PATTERN
Bounder/Indirect
COMPRESSION SHAPE
Oval

30-180kg
20-40cm

WEASEL
(Mustela nivalis)

Not endangered

Trees and holes

Woodland and meadows

Nocturnal

Weasels have long cylindrical bodies with chestnut brown fur across the back and white fur underneath. They are distinguishable from the stoat by the absence of a black tip on the end of the tail.

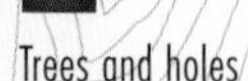

The common weasel is found throughout central and western Europe, North America, Asia and North Africa and inhabit varied habitats from sand dunes to grassland and woodland. Weasels are active during the day and at night and live in burrows which often are stolen from their prey. They feed mainly on small mammals, birds and eggs and are the smallest of all carnivores. They must feed every 24 hours or they are at risk of starvation.

Weasels are mostly solitary and scent mark their territories. Their scats are long and twisted and can be found in abundance in their dens.

Their tracks are absolutely tiny with 5 toes and sharp claws. Their high speed bounding results in sets of 4 tracks with gaps of more than 30 centimetres between them. When weasels are stalking prey or are scared they will walk slowly resulting in clear individual tracks with a stride of only 10 centimetres.

40-70kg
15-25cm

TRACKER'S TIP
Weasels (and stoats) kill their prey by biting the back of its neck. If you look carefully at any carcasses you come across this bite could well be apparent.

MINK
(Mustela vison)

Not endangered

Waterside

Waterside habitats

Nocturnal

Mink are related to stoats and weasels. They are aquatic mammals that live near rivers, streams, ponds, and lakes and their tracks can be found where the water meets the shore. They eat fish, frogs, insects, mice, birds, and amphibians.

Mink were farmed in the UK for their fur and escapees over the years have formed a solid population whose ecological niche overlaps that of the otter. Often it is possible to find signs of the two species side by side on a boundary line between their territories.

Mink have five toes on both front and hind feet. The front track, however, sometimes shows only four toes. Tracks are a bit more than an inch long.

Mink are usually nocturnal, but are occasionally active during the day. They are solitary animals which usually hunt alone. They make their nests in existing burrows by the waterside often among tree roots, or in old rabbit burrows. Mink do not hibernate in the winter. They continue to hunt, sometimes even travelling under ice that has formed on the surface of the water.

Males are highly territorial and will not tolerate other males within their range. When one is removed, another quickly occupies the vacant area.

0.5-1.7kg
45-80cm

TRACKER'S TIP
Mink scat has a particularly offensive smell, similar to rotting meat and burnt rubber, which makes it easily distinguishable from that of otters and has earned them the nickname of stinky mink!

PINE MARTEN
(Martes martes)

Pine martens are elusive nocturnal mammals which are found in pine forests and rocky scree areas. Suitable refuge sites include rocky crevices, disused squirrel nests (dreys) and holes in trees. Their fur is dark brown to black in colour with conspicuous creamy-orange throat patches. They have a pointed muzzle, prominent ears and a bushy tail. From head to tail adults are 64-81cm (25-32 inches) long. They weigh 1.3-1.7kg (2.8-3.7lb).

Feeding Pine martens are excellent climbers, and climb with agility in a squirrel-like manner from tree to tree as they search for food sources (such as birds, squirrels, rodents, rabbits, eggs, beetles, berries and even honey). They may also track down food on the ground where they are equally at home as in the trees.

Pine marten signs: Tracks and droppings indicate the presence of pine martens. Their foot prints are round and cat-like with five toes; claw prints are normally absent as they are only visible in soft ground. Droppings containing hair and feathers are deposited in regular latrines near to a boulder or log.

0.9-2.3kg
64-80cm
(incl tail)

HEDGEHOG

(Erinaceus)

Not endangered

Garden vegetation and hedges

Gardens and hedgerows

Nocturnal

Hedgehogs are native to mainland Britain and are also found throughout northern and western Europe. They are also found in north Africa, the Middle East and central Asia.

Hedgehogs are the only British mammal covered in spines. Each hedgehog has as many as 7,000 spines covering its back and sides, and when threatened, it curls into a ball, so that the spines offer protection. The chest and belly are covered in coarse grey-brown fur.

They have powerful front feet and claws for digging for slugs and worms. Surprisingly they can also climb, swim and sprint at a speed of 6 mph!

Hedgehogs hibernate alone from November to April under a supporting structure such as wood piles, brambles or compost heaps or sheds. Beetles, caterpillars and other insects, worms, frogs, bird's eggs, young birds and mammals. During the summer months hedgehogs build nests of moss and leaves in under vegetation, or in banks.

Hedgehogs live in parks, gardens and farmland. They prefer woodland edges, hedgerows and suburban gardens where food is plentiful. Tracks show 5 toes and droppings are long and cylindrical with rounded ends and no odour.

600-800g
18-13cm

TRACKER'S TIP
Watch out for tracks in flower beds where hedgehogs can often be found digging for slugs. Put down cat food to attract them to your garden.

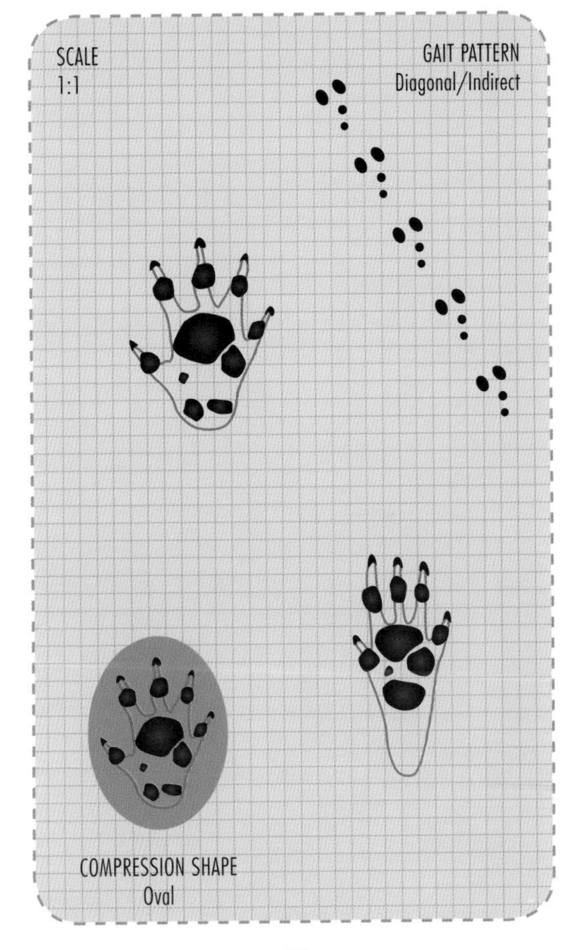

RED SQUIRREL
(Tamiasciurus hudsonicus)

Special Concern

Drey

Forest and woodlands

50-260g
20-40cm

Also known as the 'pine squirrel', the red squirrel is a familiar sight in many parts of the world. However, in some parts of the world it is being displaced by the pushy North American Gray squirrel, which has developed an interesting ecological niche of its own.

Red squirrels eat nuts, fruit and even insects and bird eggs. They can be seen running along tree trunks and leaping from branch to branch. When it reaches the ground, the red squirrel usually gallops for most of the time. Sometimes, to signify threat, it will walk slowly and 'pace'. Often lawns and ground are dug up by these squirrels as they hide nuts and then go back to retrieve them later.

The Red squirrel usually has two types of nest - the outside nest, and one inside a tree trunk often occupying disused woodpecker holes. The outside nest can be about a foot in diameter, and is more common in coniferous forest where hollow trees are in short supply. They also nest in the ground with a well concealed entrance. Red squirrels are mostly active during the day, but are also known to forage at night.

They are highly territorial and range for about 200 to 300 yards. Often a midden or perhaps a pile of cones scales and nutshells are left behind after many years of feeding in a favourite place.

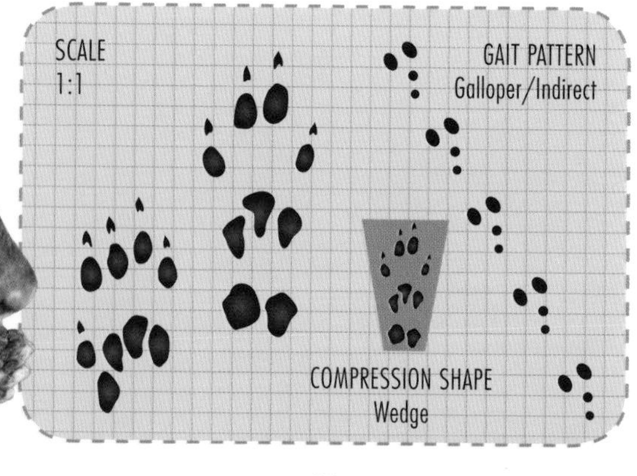

GREY SQUIRREL
(Sciurus carolinensis)

The Grey Squirrel is common throughout Europe and Britain. It is easily spotted and frequents most wooded areas. The winter fur is quite dense and is silver grey. The summer fur is yellowish brown with white underparts. They have bushy tails and no tufts on their ears.

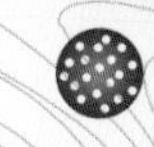

Not endangered

Drey

They have created an ecological niche and dominate the red squirrel because they do not hibernate and beat the red squirrel to the food sources.

They are very bold and territorial. They communicate by tail movements, when agitated they shake the tail. They also vocalise their territorial warnings.

They build nests in trees about the size of a football.

Forest and woodland

300-700g
38-52cm

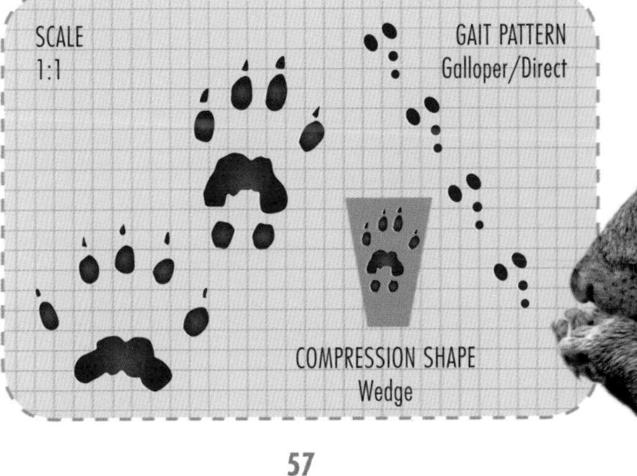

HOUSE MOUSE
(Mus musculus)

Special concern

Holes and nests

Widespread

Nocturnal

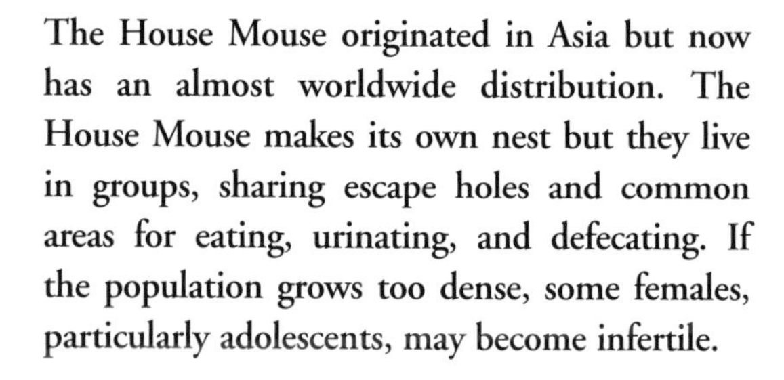

The House Mouse originated in Asia but now has an almost worldwide distribution. The House Mouse makes its own nest but they live in groups, sharing escape holes and common areas for eating, urinating, and defecating. If the population grows too dense, some females, particularly adolescents, may become infertile.

The high rate of reproduction plus its ability to migrate readily allows the house mouse to take advantage of temporary habitats not so easily available to other species such as cultivated fields. As a crop develops, the mice move in and have several litters in quick succession, building large populations quickly, then when the field is harvested or plowed, they move out.

The house mouse will often choose to live in buildings, hence its name. They can be extremely destructive, chewing furniture and wires, and sometimes start fires. They can scurry up rough vertical walls and even pipes and they gnaw holes in walls, floors, and baseboards.

The house mouse is a nocturnal animal. They will eat almost anything but have a definite preference for cereals and insects. When walking, house mouse tracks point outwards slightly and it is usually possible to see a trail where the tail has dragged along the ground. They can jump distances of up to 50 centimetres.

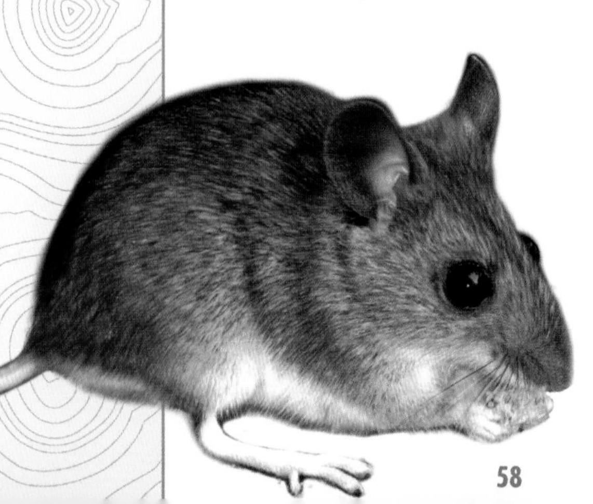

15-50g
6-15cm

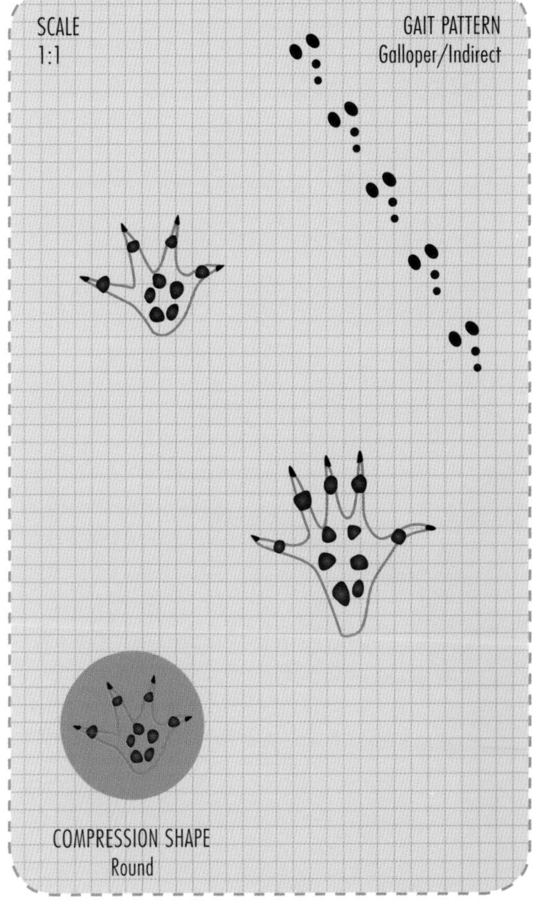
SCALE
1:1
GAIT PATTERN
Galloper/Indirect
COMPRESSION SHAPE
Round

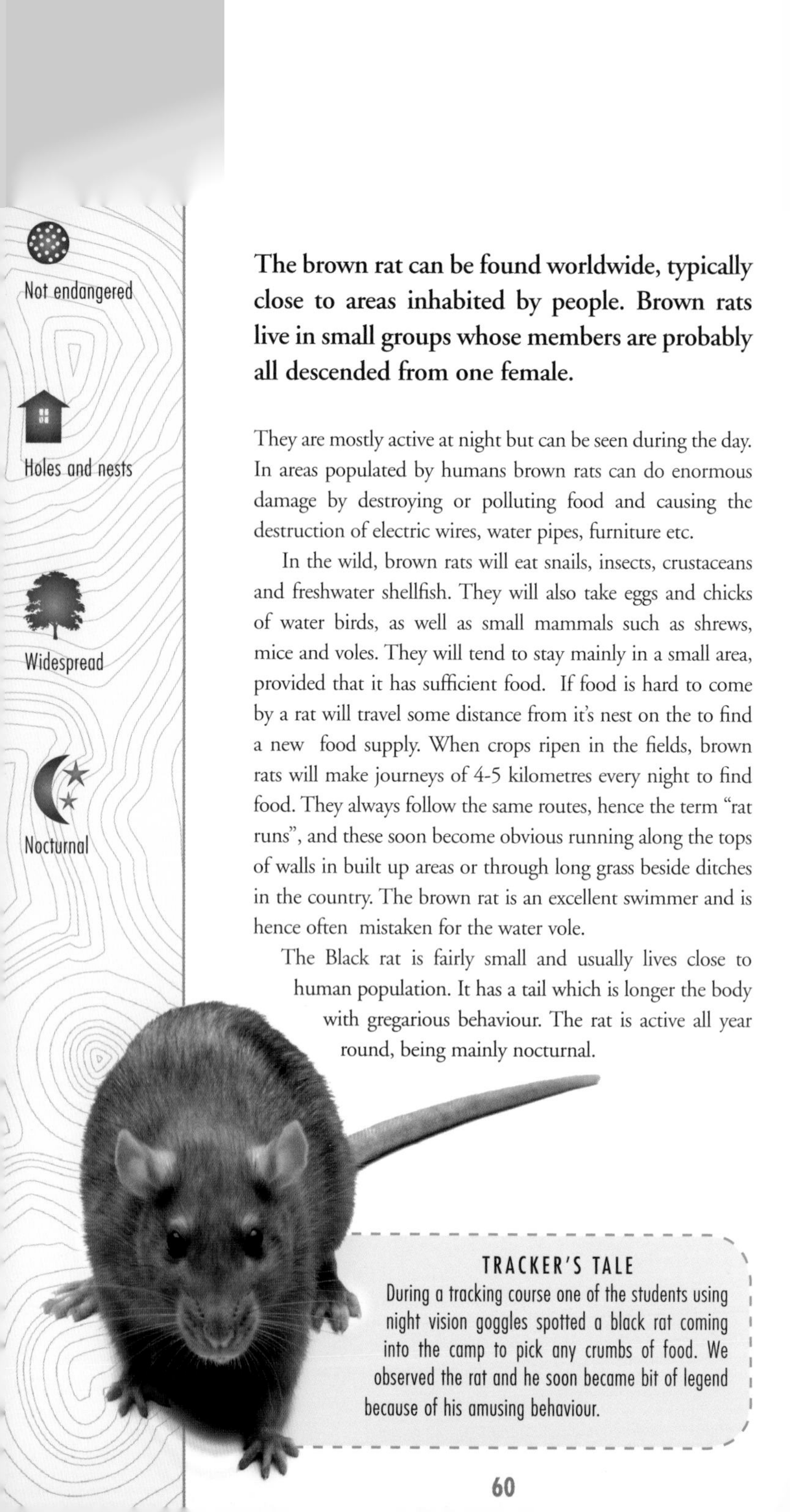

The brown rat can be found worldwide, typically close to areas inhabited by people. Brown rats live in small groups whose members are probably all descended from one female.

They are mostly active at night but can be seen during the day. In areas populated by humans brown rats can do enormous damage by destroying or polluting food and causing the destruction of electric wires, water pipes, furniture etc.

In the wild, brown rats will eat snails, insects, crustaceans and freshwater shellfish. They will also take eggs and chicks of water birds, as well as small mammals such as shrews, mice and voles. They will tend to stay mainly in a small area, provided that it has sufficient food. If food is hard to come by a rat will travel some distance from it's nest on the to find a new food supply. When crops ripen in the fields, brown rats will make journeys of 4-5 kilometres every night to find food. They always follow the same routes, hence the term "rat runs", and these soon become obvious running along the tops of walls in built up areas or through long grass beside ditches in the country. The brown rat is an excellent swimmer and is hence often mistaken for the water vole.

The Black rat is fairly small and usually lives close to human population. It has a tail which is longer the body with gregarious behaviour. The rat is active all year round, being mainly nocturnal.

TRACKER'S TALE

During a tracking course one of the students using night vision goggles spotted a black rat coming into the camp to pick any crumbs of food. We observed the rat and he soon became bit of legend because of his amusing behaviour.

100-500g
20-30cm

TRACKER'S TIP
Watch for tail drag which is characteristic trait of the rat. Brown rat tracks show a long heel area on the hind foot. There is hardly ever a drag line created by the tail.

RABBIT
(Oryctolagus cuniculus)

Not endangered

Holes

Open fields

0.9-1.4kg
20-40cm

Nocturnal

The rabbit is found throughout Europe and can often be seen at dawn and dusk. They are gregarious in their behaviour and live in large underground burrows.

The prints usually show claw marks, the front pads being smaller and rounder than the back pads that resemble a slipper –shaped impression. Rabbits have a fifth pad which rarely shows.

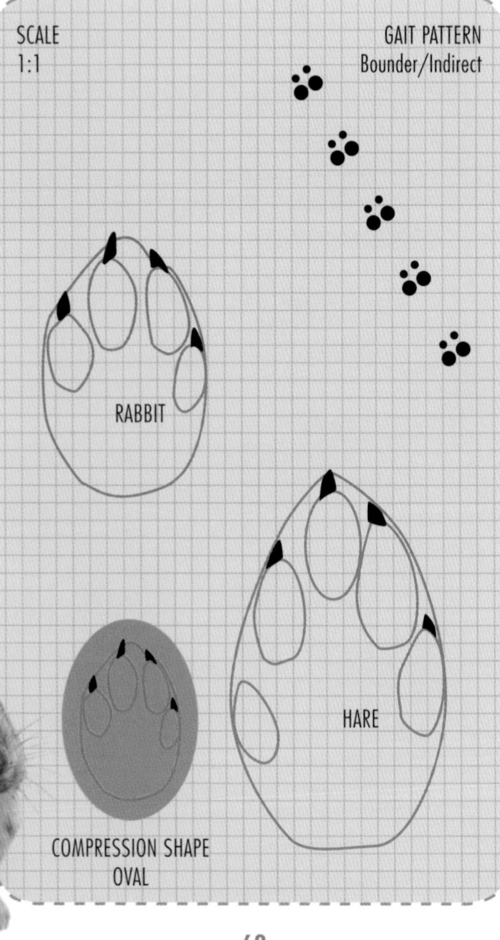

HARE
(Lepus capensis)

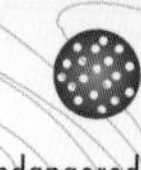
Not endangered

Holes

Open fields

1.4-5.9kg
33-70cm

Nocturnal

Brown Hare have colonised cultivated landscapes and displaced the Mountain Hare or Blue Hare, which in Britain is now mostly confined to upland areas. They are born above ground with a full coat of fur. Adult Brown Hares are considerably larger than rabbits, with very long black-tipped ears, powerful hind legs. Hares can grow to a length of about 70 cm from their nose to the tip of their tail.

The Brown Hare lives in territories on open downland and farms. They feed mainly on grass, roots, bark and the produce of farms and gardens and require this diversity of food.

The Blue or Mountain Hare is smaller than the Brown Hare and lives in the mountainous areas of Scotland, the Peak District and North Wales. During the winter their coats turn white to camouflage themselves in snow.

Brown Hare live in very exposed habitats and relying upon acute senses and can run at speeds of up to 70kph to evade predators. Hare make a small depression on the ground among long grass - a form - where they spend most of their day, moving out into open ground to feed at night.

The 'boxing' behaviour associated with 'Mad March Hares' is usually a female fighting off the attentions of a male. The young, known as leverets, are born fully formed with their eyes open. They receive little parental care and are left alone in a form throughout the day; the mother only returning at sunset to feed the young.

WATER VOLE
(Arvicola terrestris)

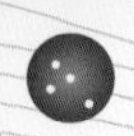

Special concern

Holes and nests

Riverside habitats

Nocturnal

The water vole has four prominent toes that show claws clearly on the front foot and five on the back foot.

Watch out for roots that have been gnawed and trees debarked in the summer, this is exclusive to ash trees. The wood underneath will look rough with lots of tooth marks and will be within 15 to 20cms of the ground as the water vole cannot climb.

The Bank vole tracks are similar to the Water Vole and is widely distributed. It is active day and night, making well worn, extensive trails. It is also a climber and will go into trees and bushes.

200-300g
20-32cm
(incl tail)

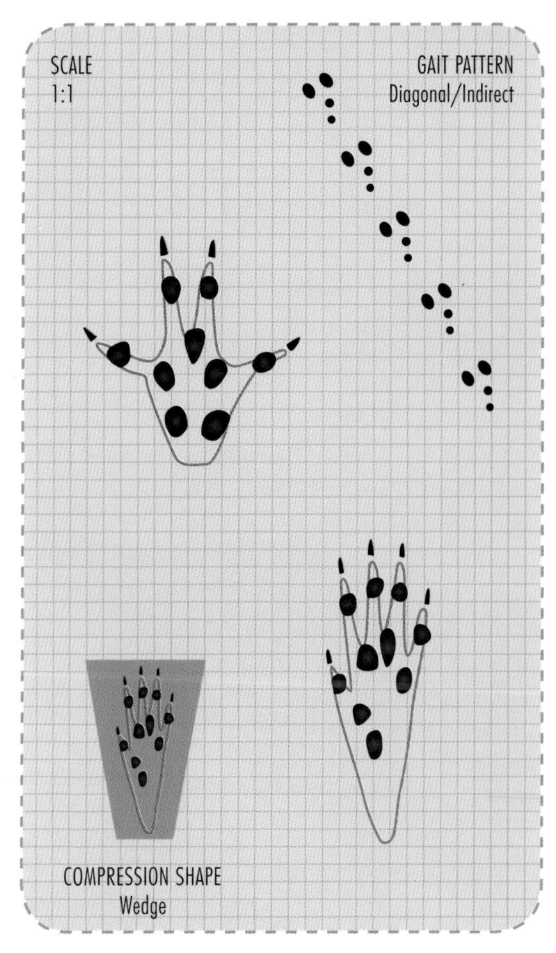

COMMON SHREW
(Sorex araneus)

Known as sharp nosed mice, they are always busy trying to find insects to eat. The tracks of shrew are hard to find, but can sometimes be seen in fine dust or soft mud. It is widely distributed and favors nesting under logs and vegetation. It tunnels through leaves to find food.

The Pygmy Shrew is similar to the Common Shrew but tunnels less than the Common Shrew. It is widespread and is a very good climber.

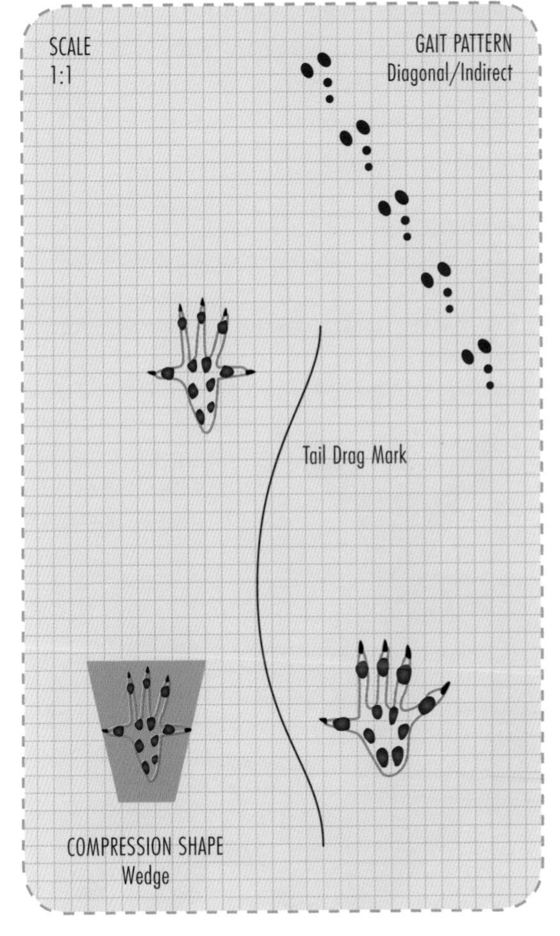

SCALE
1:1
GAIT PATTERN
Diagonal/Indirect
Tail Drag Mark
COMPRESSION SHAPE
Wedge

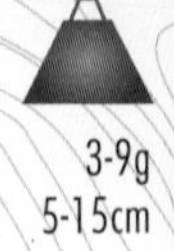

3-9g
5-15cm

Roe deer is indigenous to the British Isles. The summer coat of both male and female is chestnut red and during the winter months the coat colour is more grey or dark brown. Roe deer have a white rump with virtually no tail at all. When shedding the velvet from the antlers damage is caused to young trees by males. Further damage is caused from April onwards as mature bucks begin to mark out their territories. The bark is stripped and scent is deposited onto the wet sapwood underneath. Roe are herbivores and can be found in a wide variety of habitats, ranging from open moor to thick cover in conifer or deciduous woodland.

Roe like to sunbathe and a sunlit clearing in cover will often be a favourite place to lie up. A telltale sign of this would be a depression in vegetation.

Roe have an excellent sense of smell but their eyesight is limited and they can only see in shades of black and white. They are however able to detect the slightest physical movement and can spot a moving human form at considerable distances.

Tracks are small slender and narrow towards the front and can look almost heart shaped.

18-28kg
68cm-1.5m

TRACKER'S TIP
It is common to see dew claws in the tracks of Roe Deer when they are moving at speed or walking over soft ground.

RED DEER
(Cervus elaphus)

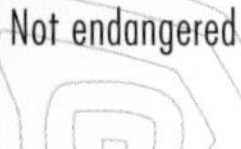

Not endangered

Coniferous forest and heathland

The Red Deer is Britain's largest native land mammal, standing up to 1.5m at the shoulder. Red deer are dark red or brown in the summer months with a lighter cream underbelly, inner thighs and rump. Sometimes spots are visible on the coat, particularly along the spine. In the winter the coat changes to a darker brown or grey, with lighter patches on the rump and undersides.

They usually stay in single-sex groups for most of the year, coming together for mating during the October 'rut'.

Red deer are mainly forest dwellers, but they are highly adaptive and they will move into areas with higher availability of food. Red deer tend to spend the night in lower, more sheltered areas and move to higher sunny slopes where they spend the day resting and feeding. These daytime resting areas will normally be good vantage points from which they can easily see approaching danger. New-born calves are often left in patches of bracken or nettles by their mothers, who will return periodically to feed them. Red deer are grazers, however good grass is not always available so many other food sources are taken advantage of including rough grasses, heather and dwarf shrubs. Tracks are fairly large with broad cleaves and distinct toe pads.

TRACKER'S TALE

When tracking otters up a stream one day I came across the antlers of two red deer which were completely tangled together with twine. The pair seemed to have met an unfortunate end in a fight which had resulted in them being tied together and unable to separate.

TRACKER'S TIP
Red deer will strip the bark from trees up to 2 metres high in winter and spring. They particularly favour conifers.

FALLOW DEER
(Dama dama)

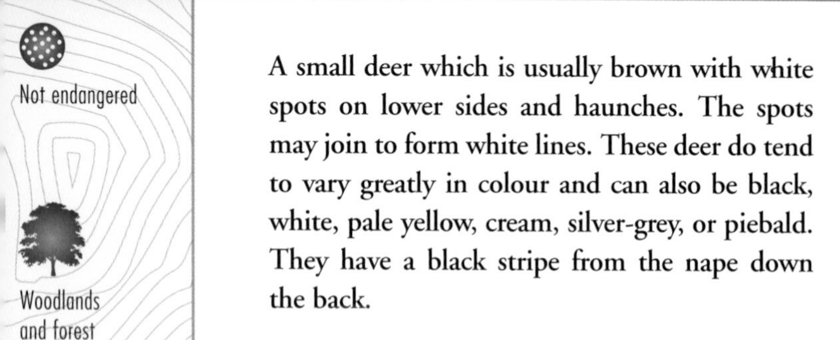

A small deer which is usually brown with white spots on lower sides and haunches. The spots may join to form white lines. These deer do tend to vary greatly in colour and can also be black, white, pale yellow, cream, silver-grey, or piebald. They have a black stripe from the nape down the back.

The hind legs are slightly longer than the forelegs, so that the rump is held high and the short neck has a prominent larynx. The dewclaws are very small and high on the legs.

Fallow Deer run in a peculiar stiff-legged fashion, bouncing along as if on a pogo stick and when they are disturbed they will occasionally bound away in a manner known as pronking. This consists of all four feet being brought together and then leaving the ground simultaneously as the animal flees. Fallow deer graze on grasses and herbaceous plants in summer, and browse on the woody parts of deciduous trees and conifers in winter. In areas with high numbers of these deer it is sometimes possible to see a browse line on vegetation around 2 metres from the ground. Fallow do not establish a territory but will have a large home range. Within this home range will be areas that are used more often than others.

35-95kg
1-2m

TRACKER'S TIP
Sometimes the raised areas are the only part of the track to show, especially the tips which are often unequal lengths.

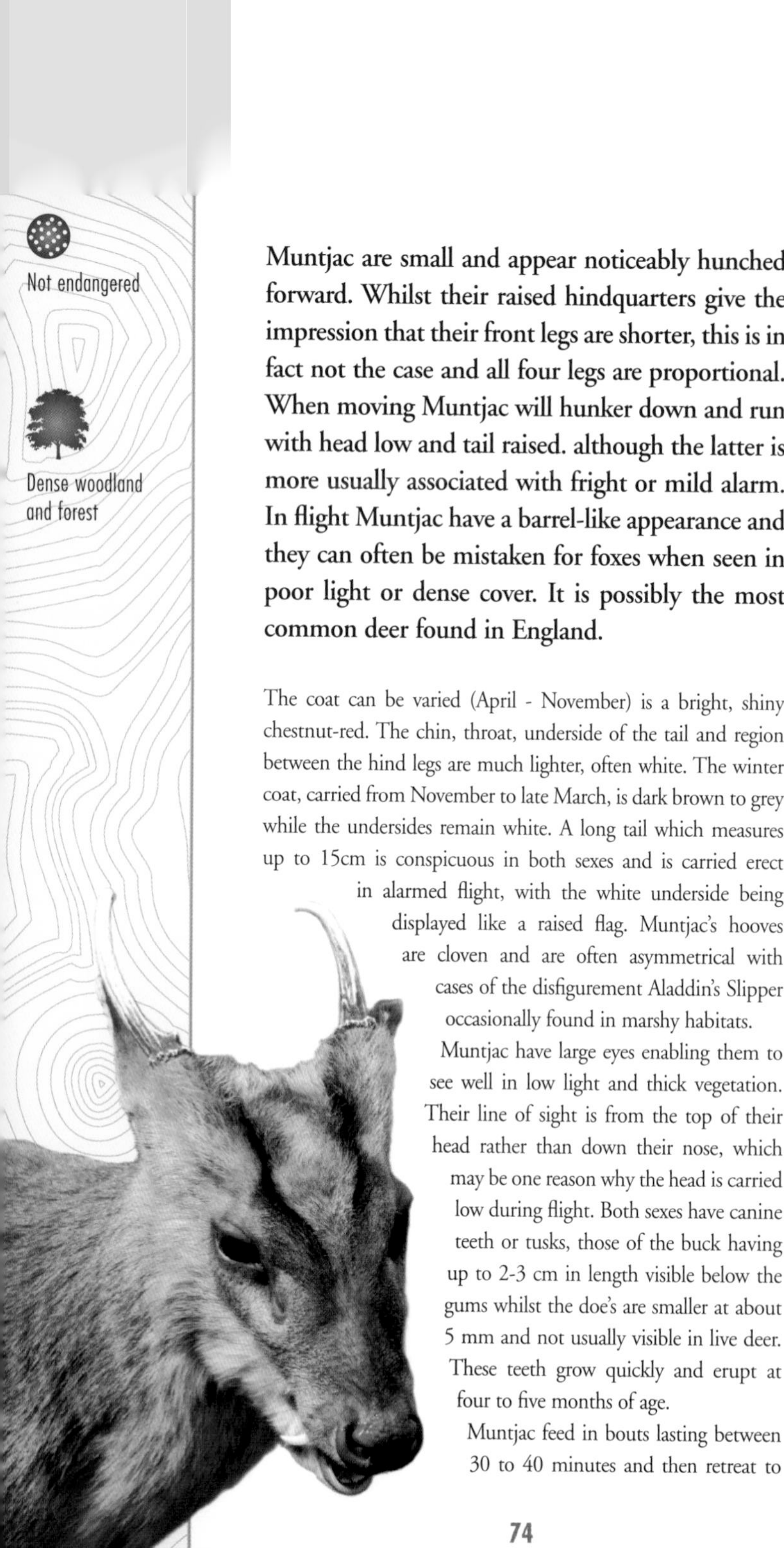

Muntjac are small and appear noticeably hunched forward. Whilst their raised hindquarters give the impression that their front legs are shorter, this is in fact not the case and all four legs are proportional. When moving Muntjac will hunker down and run with head low and tail raised. although the latter is more usually associated with fright or mild alarm. In flight Muntjac have a barrel-like appearance and they can often be mistaken for foxes when seen in poor light or dense cover. It is possibly the most common deer found in England.

The coat can be varied (April - November) is a bright, shiny chestnut-red. The chin, throat, underside of the tail and region between the hind legs are much lighter, often white. The winter coat, carried from November to late March, is dark brown to grey while the undersides remain white. A long tail which measures up to 15cm is conspicuous in both sexes and is carried erect in alarmed flight, with the white underside being displayed like a raised flag. Muntjac's hooves are cloven and are often asymmetrical with cases of the disfigurement Aladdin's Slipper occasionally found in marshy habitats.

Muntjac have large eyes enabling them to see well in low light and thick vegetation. Their line of sight is from the top of their head rather than down their nose, which may be one reason why the head is carried low during flight. Both sexes have canine teeth or tusks, those of the buck having up to 2-3 cm in length visible below the gums whilst the doe's are smaller at about 5 mm and not usually visible in live deer. These teeth grow quickly and erupt at four to five months of age.

Muntjac feed in bouts lasting between 30 to 40 minutes and then retreat to cover to digest and you may see push-downs in the grass where it has layn down. Predominantly browsers, they will take advantage of their diverse habitats, readily eating ivy, bramble, grasses, herbs, fruit (especially apples), nuts, berries, fungi, flowers (both wild and cultivated), vegetables and coppice. They will also eat some plants poisonous to domestic animals, including Yew leaves, berries and bluebells.

As other mammals increasingly encroach upon urban areas, it is a point of conjecture that the Muntjac could quite rapidly become the established urban deer in Britain.

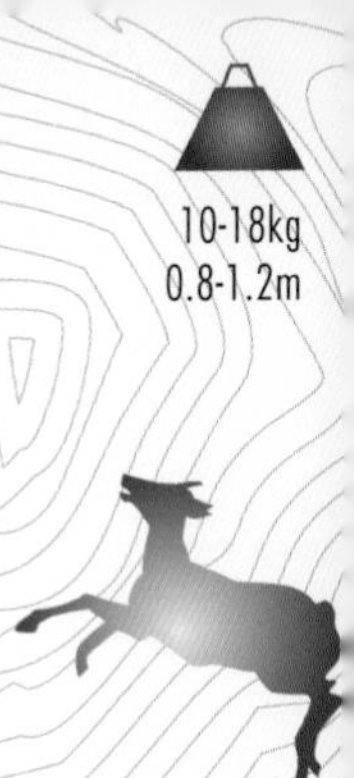

TRACKER'S TIP
Sometimes the raised areas are the only part of the track to show, especially the tips which are often unequal lengths.

CHINESE WATER DEER
(Hydropotes inermis)

Not endangered

Reed beds, swamps and marsh

11-18kg
0.8-1.2m

Adult male Chinese Water Deer (bucks) stand in the region of 50-55cm at the shoulder, with the females (does) about 3-5cm shorter. The adult water deer can perhaps best be visualized as being between the sizes of a Roe deer and a Muntjac.

The hind legs of the Chinese Water Deer are longer than the fore legs which causes the rump to be carried higher than the shoulder, without appearing hunched up. It is this high rump feature which assists in distinguishing these deer from Muntjac does. However, they can be more easily mistaken for Roe does and Canine teeth or tusks are grown by both bucks and does and these usually erupt in the autumn of the deer's first year at approximately 6-7 months of age. Bucks' tusks are considerably longer than does'.

When two bucks are fighting they leave scuff marks in the ground and some fur may be left behind.

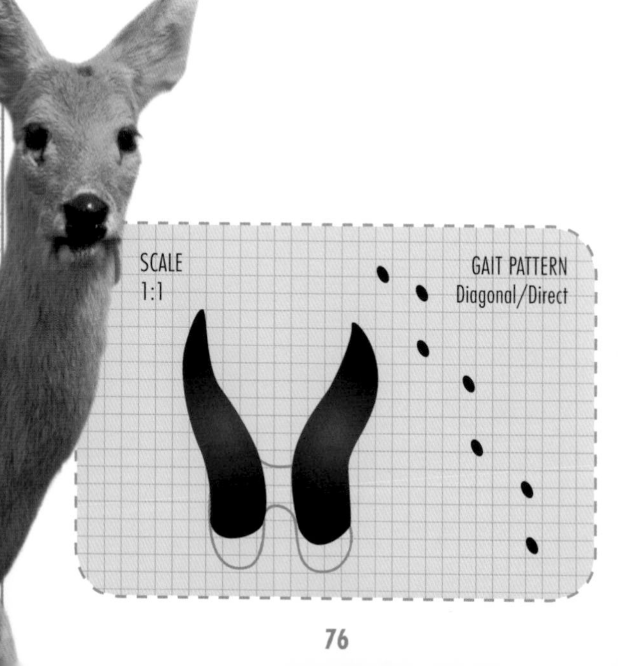

SIKA DEER
(Cervus nippon)

Sika Deer are a small elk and live in the New Forest, Dorset and Scotland. They are about 1m high at the shoulder, weigh 30-70 kilos and originate from Asia (China, Japan, Korea, Taiwan). The sika deer coat is dark brown to black. Some have faint white parallel spots on their back. They also have a white rump. Males are larger than females and have large antlers. Males also have a dark shaggy mane running down their neck.

Not endangered

Damp woodland and heathland

30-70kg
0.8-1.3m

Sika are predominantly grazers, feeding heavily on grasses, broadleaf buds and twigs, heather, fruits, fungi and acornsone would expect to see these crepuscular (meaning preference for twilight) animals in the last two hours of daylight or during the first hour after dawn on their way to and from their feeding

Territories are marked by a stag thrashing the ground cover of heather and gorse with his antlers, leaving circular patches at intervals along the boundaries and some fraying of perimeter trees. Fighting between stags is commonplace

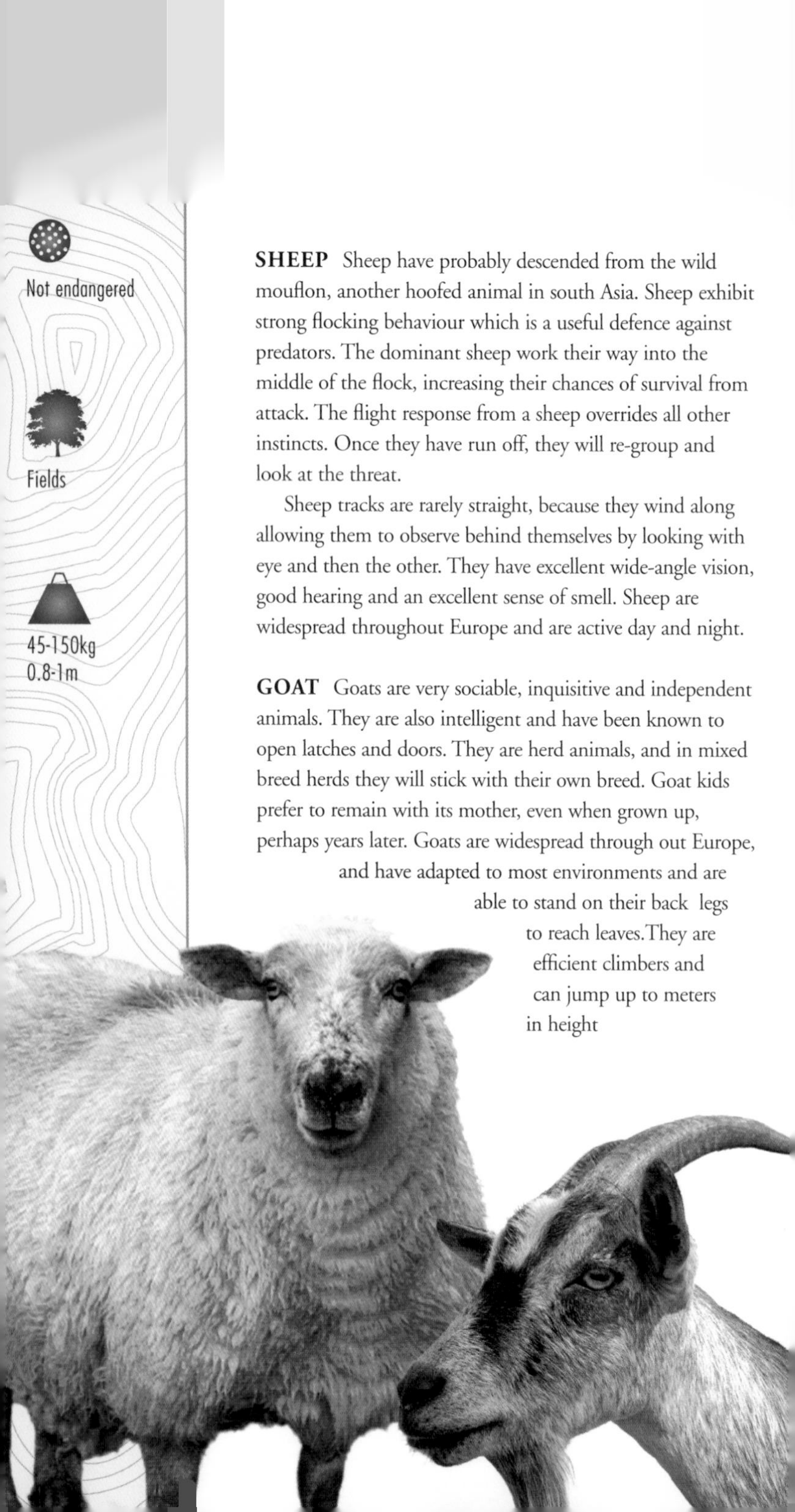

SHEEP Sheep have probably descended from the wild mouflon, another hoofed animal in south Asia. Sheep exhibit strong flocking behaviour which is a useful defence against predators. The dominant sheep work their way into the middle of the flock, increasing their chances of survival from attack. The flight response from a sheep overrides all other instincts. Once they have run off, they will re-group and look at the threat.

Sheep tracks are rarely straight, because they wind along allowing them to observe behind themselves by looking with eye and then the other. They have excellent wide-angle vision, good hearing and an excellent sense of smell. Sheep are widespread throughout Europe and are active day and night.

GOAT Goats are very sociable, inquisitive and independent animals. They are also intelligent and have been known to open latches and doors. They are herd animals, and in mixed breed herds they will stick with their own breed. Goat kids prefer to remain with its mother, even when grown up, perhaps years later. Goats are widespread through out Europe, and have adapted to most environments and are able to stand on their back legs to reach leaves.They are efficient climbers and can jump up to meters in height

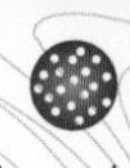

Not endangered

Fields

10-110kgs
0.4-1.2m

TRACKER'S TIP
I have been called to track the culprit for sheep kills. Usually the offender is dogs, sometimes badger, but is also the more sinister large cats roaming the British countryside.

WILD BOAR

Not endangered

Muddy areas

Dense woodland and forest

50-200kg
0.9-1.8m

Tracks of wild boar are found throughout Europe and making a come-back to the UK as the result of captive Polish Boars escaping into the wild. There appears to be high populations in Dorset and Hampshire. They are usually to be found in thick forest but can also be found in arid areas although they tend to stay near to small river valleys and muddy wallows. Often these areas are very difficult to access and going into a wallow can be dangerous as the boar may panic and charge anything in its way.

Occasionally boar will come out of the overgrown areas and although their tracks resemble those of domestic pig they are easily identified from that of deer and other animals. The tracks of wild boar and pig show pointed dew claws in the ground, however the trail of a wild boar is narrow and may go through terrain that a domestic pig would not be able to do. They are also very agile and will cross water using a fallen tree.

Look for giveaway rooted up earth rubs against trees that will likely leave coarse hair on the tree. The muddied area on the tree will indicate the height which can be up to 1 metre high.

SCALE
1:2
GAIT PATTERN
Diagonal/Indirect
COMPRESSION SHAPE
Oval

HORSE

Not endangered

Fields and bridleways

700kg
2m

Horse tracks are easy to distinguish. There are two types. The wild horse, without a shoe and the shod horse. The wild horse track is a single round or oval hoof with a distinct v mark in the middle. The shod horse will make a single mark with the iron rim and sometimes you can see the nails that hold the shoe on.

Horse tracks can be seen everywhere, especially close to human habitation. The surprising fact is that horses hooves are actually like one big toe.

Wild horses roam freely on some moor land especially Dartmoor where the wild ponies live out a tough life in extreme weather conditions. Because they live in areas that are soft and swamp-like their hooves are surprisingly large. In some areas of Europe only the front hooves have iron shoes.

WILD HORSE

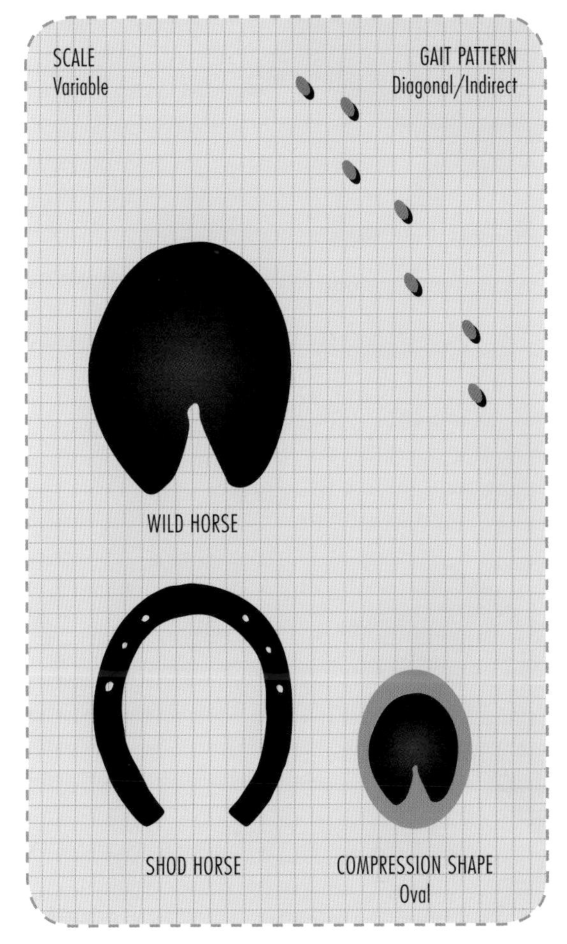

Special concern

Moorland

700kgs
2m

TRACKER'S TIP
The white rhinoceros and wild stallion horse will leave droppings in one place called a midden until a pile has accumulated as part of a territorial claim.

RAVEN & CROW

RAVEN The raven print is a large four toed track. Lobes are present, claws are very long and rounded.

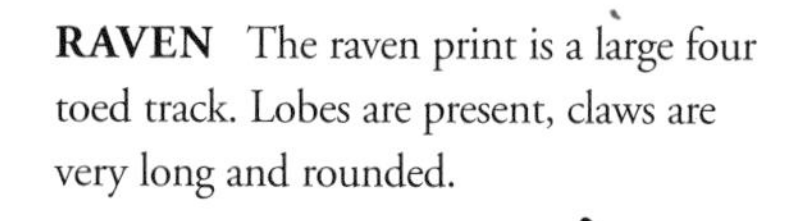

RAVEN

SCALE 1:1

CROW The crow is always four toed with the back toe being small and offset from the central line. The three forward toes have small detached claws and the back one very long and sharp.

CROW

SCALE 1:1

GOOSE Geese have three toes with concave webbing. The toe prints clearly show lobes with claws visible on the end.

GOOSE

SCALE
1:1

HERON The heron normally shows four toes and ranges from large to enormous with the front toe being very long. Toes and track point distinctly forward.

HERON

SCALE
1:1

PHEASANT & PARTRIDGE

PHEASANT The pheasant is four toed. The middle toe is much longer than the others. The back toe is small. The toes are slender and show lobes with big claws.

PHEASANT

SCALE
1:1

PARTRIDGE Four toed, assymetrical, lobes can usually be seen with small claws.

SCALE
1:1

PARTRIDGE

PLOVER & MAGPIE

PLOVER The Plover has three toes, which are slightly asymmetric. Sometimes there is a small indentation at the base of the toes. It has very short, though blunt claws often joined to the track.

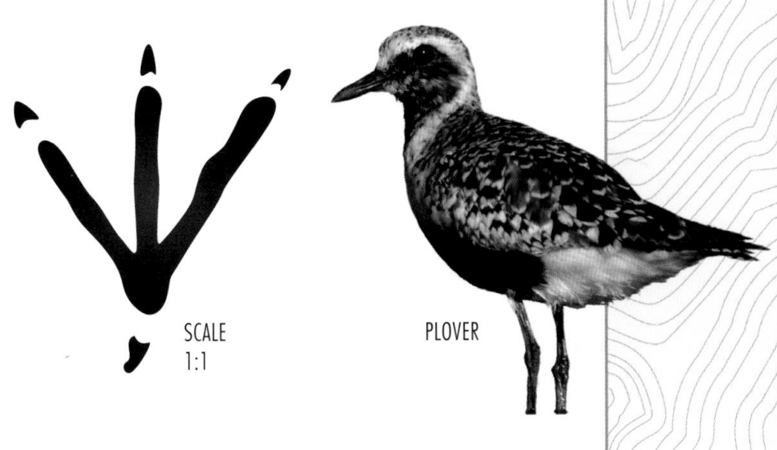

MAGPIE The magpie is a familiar sight in the UK. The tracks are asymmetrical four toed. One of the outside toes turns inwards, similar to crows. Small claw marks can be seen, detached from the toe.

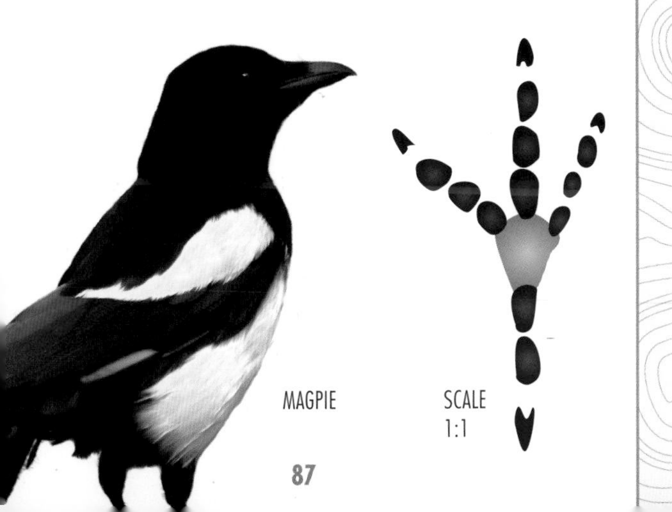

LIZARD & SNAKE

LIZARD In the UK there are two types, the sand lizard found in southern Britain and the common lizard found in most parts of the UK.

Because they are reptiles and need the suns energy they are commonly found basking on stones and will move fast when disturbed. Lizards will gorge themselves on food when it is available, eating most insects and sometimes eat their young. Sometimes lizards can be confused with newts, but if you look closer you will see that the lizard has a scaly back. The common lizard can shed its tail if attacked by a predator.

SNAKE Snakes are relatively common in the UK, especially adders that are regularly spotted in the south of England. They have good sight, taste and can feel vibrations through their auditory nerve. Most European snakes move in a serpentine style. There are three types of snakes in the UK, the adder, the grass snake and the smooth snake.

FROG Although called the common frog, it is no longer so common. It is still a familiar native amphibian. There is also the marsh frog. Frogs are around from February to October and are usually seen during the breeding season between February and March. During this time frogs can be seen in unlikely places. Frogs are different to toads because they have a moist feel and raised back. They also have no neck, with the base of the skull resting very close to the collarbone. Frogs usually hop, whereas toads prefer to walk.

TOAD Toads are a well known and familiar sight. There are two types in the UK, the common Toad and the Natterjack, which is rarely seen. Toads come out in February until October. They prefer to live in dense woodland and reasonably damp areas where there is lots of cover. Toads look different to frogs in that the skin is warty. Toads prefer to waddle rather than hop and has a rounder snout.

BADGER SETT Some badger setts are known to be over one hundred years old. They prefer to build their homes on the side of a slope so that water will run off. Setts have a distinctive shape, being wider than they are tall, with a flat bottom like a D on its back. Fox and rabbit holes are more rounded and oval in shape. Badger setts can be co-habited by rabbits, otter cats and fox at the same time.

They like sandy soil and chalk to dig their setts and often there will be several holes, the average being twelve, some giving the appearance that they are not active.

The entrance may have bedding like moss and leaves and a furrow leading into the hole. The mound of earth at the entrance will be a short distance away.

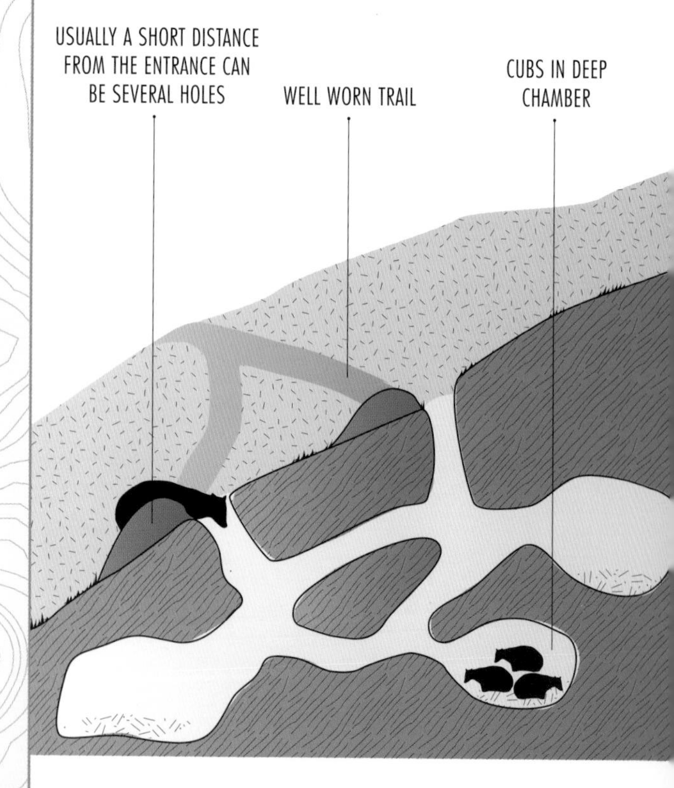

RABBIT WARREN Rabbits are highly sociable creatures and build their homes with inter-connecting tunnels with many holes. Some of the excavations can leave large piles of earth and sand at the entrance, however some tunnels are dug from the inside, with the earth being pushed backwards so no earth is visible at the entrance. Some well established warrens can resemble a fox earth, however there will be dried up rabbit droppings near the entrance and will not have a strong smell, characteristic of the fox earth.

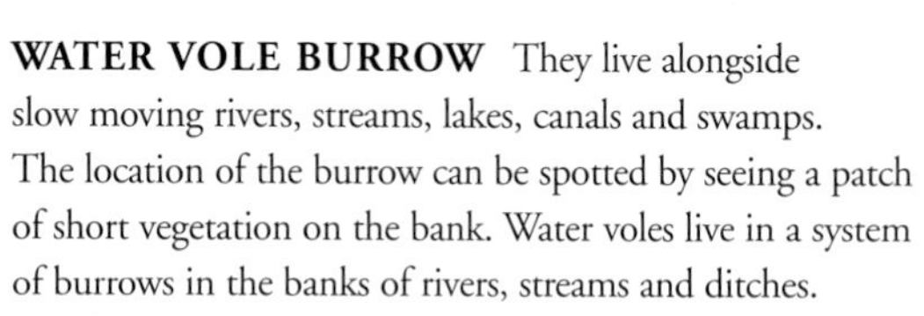

WATER VOLE BURROW They live alongside slow moving rivers, streams, lakes, canals and swamps. The location of the burrow can be spotted by seeing a patch of short vegetation on the bank. Water voles live in a system of burrows in the banks of rivers, streams and ditches.

The amount of bank-side and vegetation is important as it provides both cover and food. The entrance to their burrow is usually underwater, however sometimes the tunnels may be above the water and emerge on the bank where the vegetation will be obviously shorter than its surroundings.

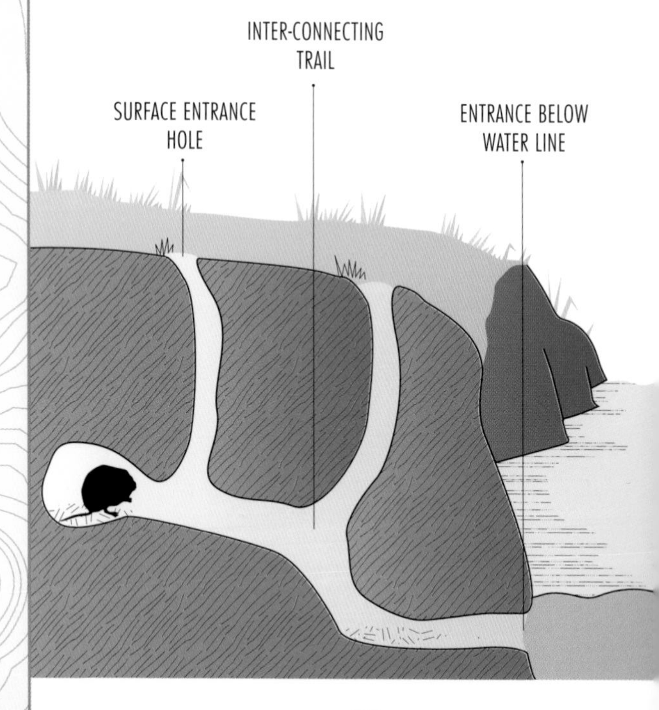

FOX DEN (EARTH) Space is a very important resource for the fox. Each family needs several safe dens sites in which to raise their cubs. They also have safe resting sites outside of the den. It is common for red foxes to have their dens inside their territory which can be three to eight kilometres.

The den can be in the form of tunnels, holes in the ground, under trees, rocks and manmade sites including building debris and pipes.

In open areas and sloping ground the fox will dig several exits and in doing so push excavated earth to the exit thus forming a fan shape at the entrance of the hole.

Some dens can be decades old and in some cases centuries, the entrance to these dens can be bigger than the usual narrow entrance of about 30cms.

An occupied den will have a strong smell, with remains of bones and feathers nearby. By products of fox including, remains of their prey cause nearby vegetation to be lush, especially the prolific growth of nettles. A fox den is taller than a badger sett.

FEEDING SIGNS It is always useful to corroborate what animal was in the area by looking at feeding signs in vegetation. By examining plants you will be able to age the presence of an animal. If the vegetation is still weeping fluids then it will be fresh. If the damage has turned brown in colour then it could be anything from a few hours old to several weeks.

1. Eaten by a carnivore, especially dog or cat family. The edge is torn.
2. Eaten by a rodent. The top edge is cut cleanly through where both teeth have incised the vegetation. Sometimes the tough outer sheath is left un-eaten.
3. Eaten by a deer. Deer have incisor teeth only on the lower jaw. The teeth are brought up and the vegetation is pressed against a tough kerratin lined upper jaw and cut, leaving an angled cut and small tassel of fibre. By looking closely at the cut you can tell where the deer was standing when it ate the plant.

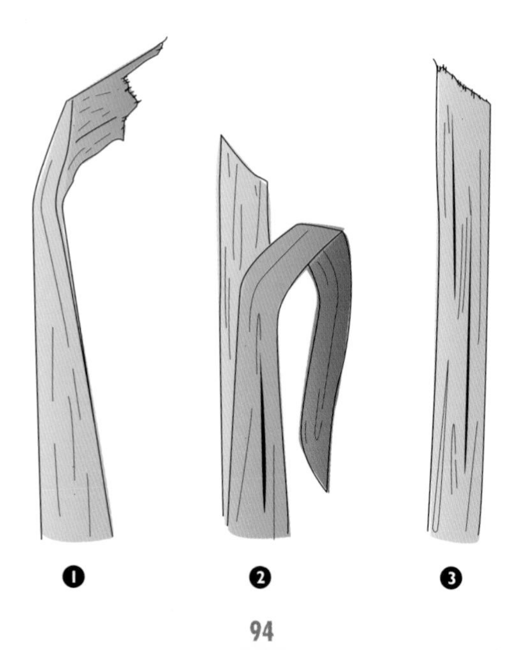

HAZLENUTS Nuts form an important part of autumn and winter diets for birds and mammals. The method of opening can identify the culprit.

1. WOODPECKER The nut is attacked lengthways showing peck marks. The bird sometimes pecks and twists which can give a rough appearance. Often woodpeckers will jam cones and nuts into rock crevices and trees. Watch out for accumulations of debris underneath the feeding place known as an anvil.
2. WATER VOLE The nut will show gnawing that commences from the side and may work upwards.
3. BANK VOLE The nut will normally show gnawing from one end of the nut, leaving a rough rimmed hole without teeth marks
4. WOOD MOUSE The nut is held between the ground and the mouse chest, tilted towards the breast. Once a mouse has got a good grip of the nut it will make a small hole. From there it will use its bottom incisors to gnaw, which will give the appearance of being eaten from the inside. The edges will show gnawing marks

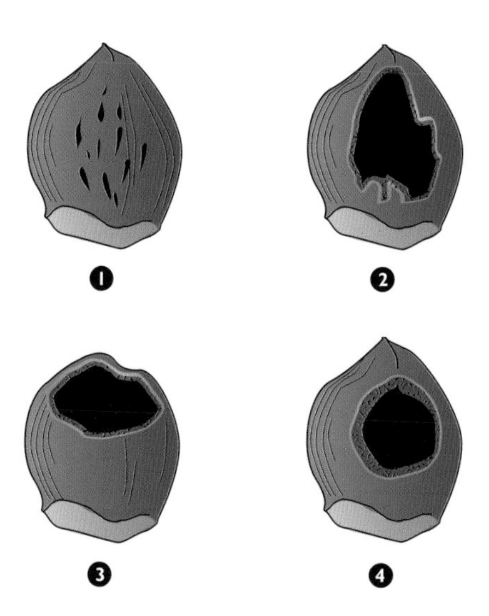

FEEDING ID

Lots of information can be gained from spotting what an animal has been eating. Trees, shrubs, fruit and grass will be damaged. Most animals prefer to eat whilst hidden and sometimes will retire to a concealed spot to digest food, deer will show distinctive indentations where they lie down.

- Deer will clip off tips of plants and sometimes strip bark from a tree. Male deer will rub their antlers against trees leaving obvious damage.
- Generally the height of the feeding signs indicates the animal. The exception is squirrel which strips bark and the woodpecker.

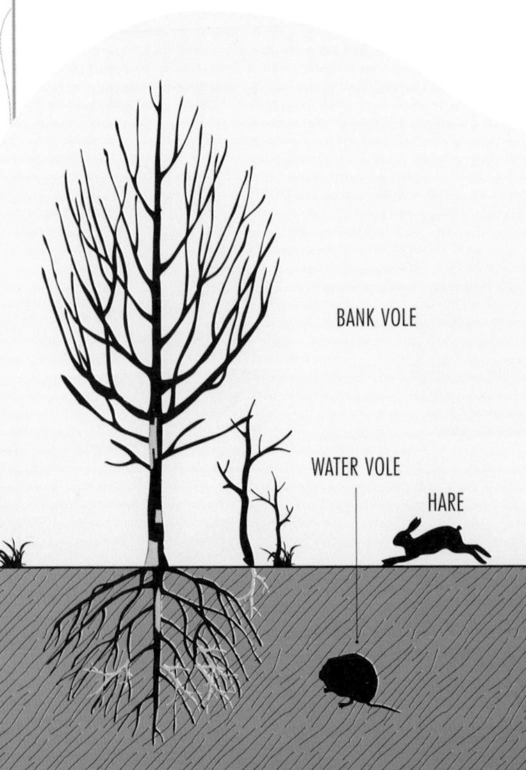

- Rodent like rabbit, hare and voles signs show clear teeth marks.
- Sheep and goats will show wear marks and some teeth marks on the bark.
- Badger sometimes climb trees to find grubs and often scratch marks can be found one to two meters off the ground where the badger has clawed its way up.

DROPPINGS ID

WATER VOLE

BROWN RAT

HOUSE MOUSE

HEDGEHOG

SCALE
1:1

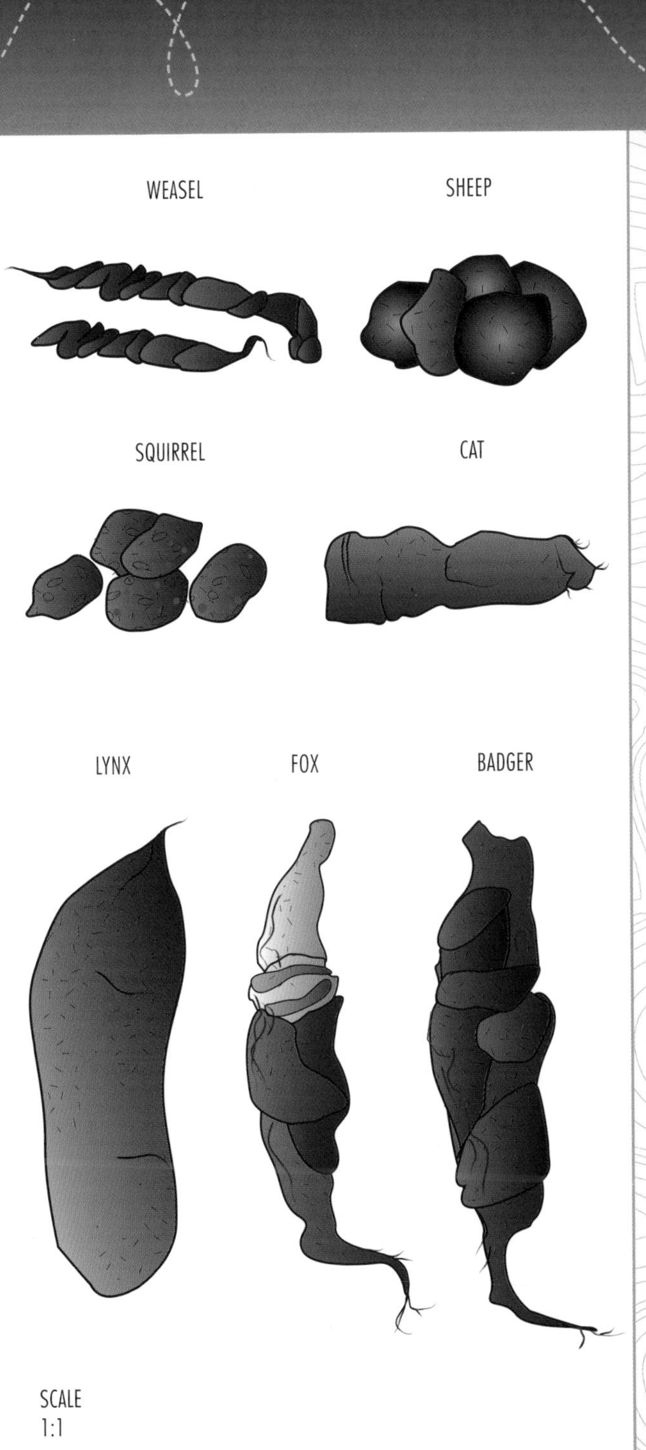
WEASEL
SHEEP
SQUIRREL
CAT
LYNX
FOX
BADGER
SCALE
1:1

SCALE
1:1

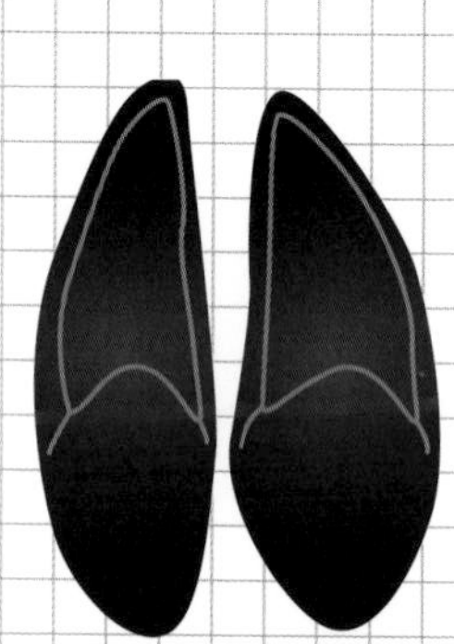

MUNTJAC

FALLOW DEER

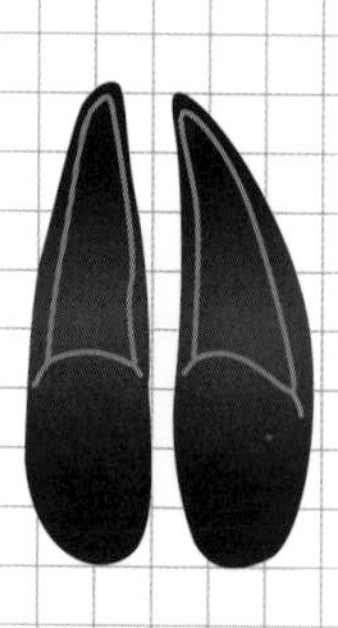

SIKA DEER

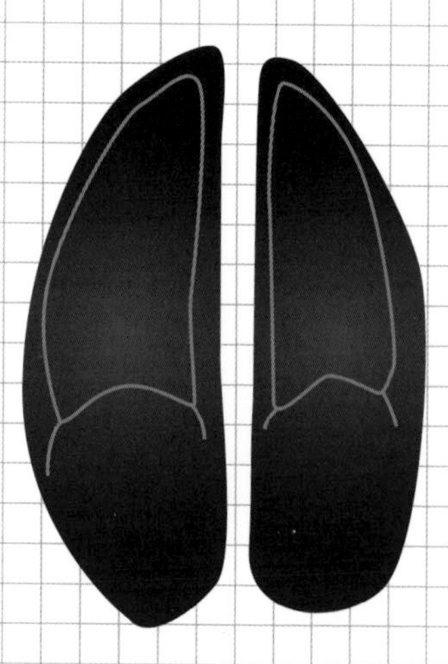

RED DEER

SCALE
1:1

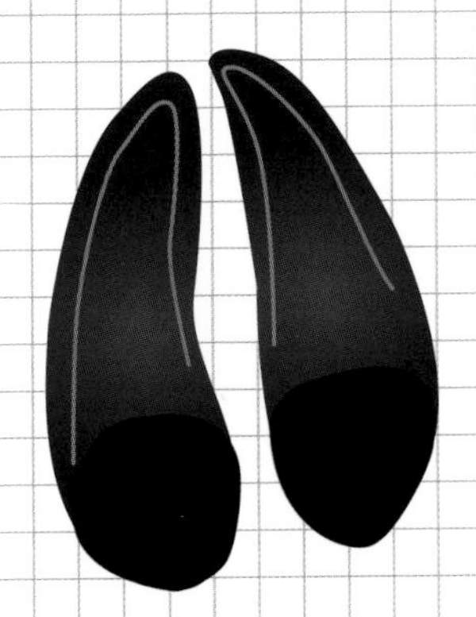

ROE DEER

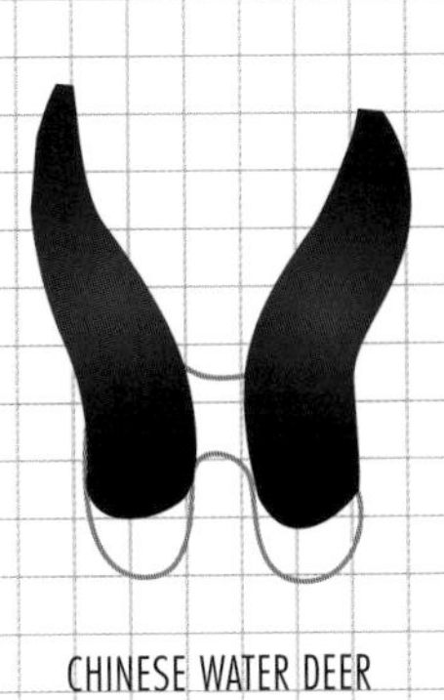

CHINESE WATER DEER

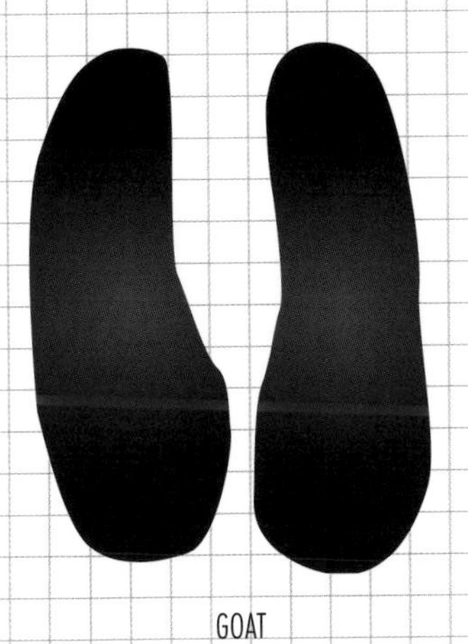

GOAT

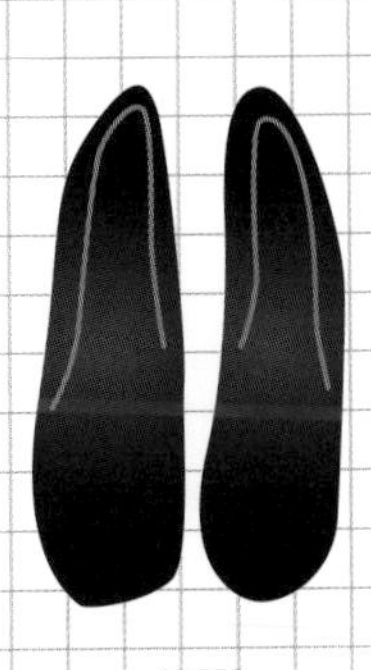

SHEEP

SCALE
1:2 (approx)

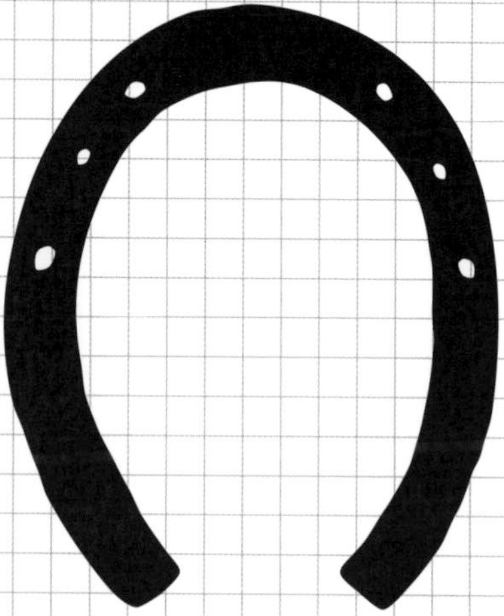

SHOD HORSE

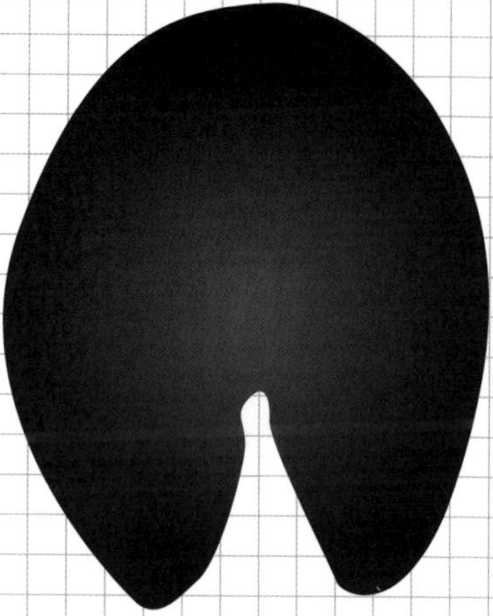

WILD HORSE

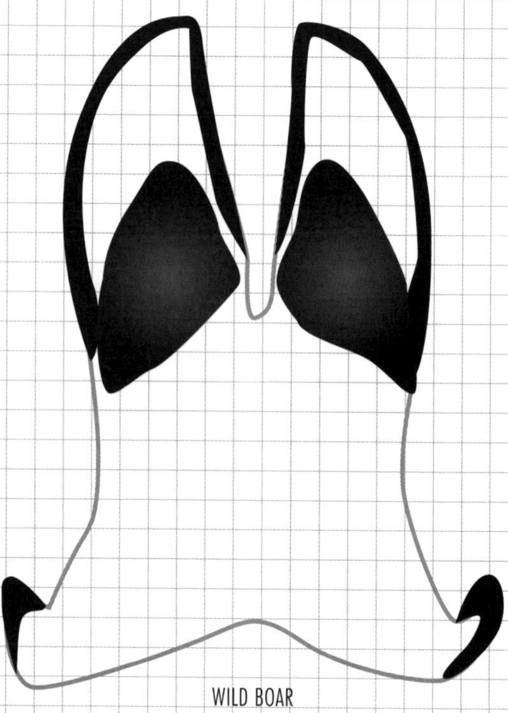

WILD BOAR

SCALE
1:1

SCALE
1:1

DOMESTIC CAT

SCALE
1:2

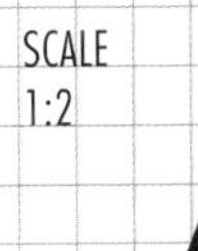

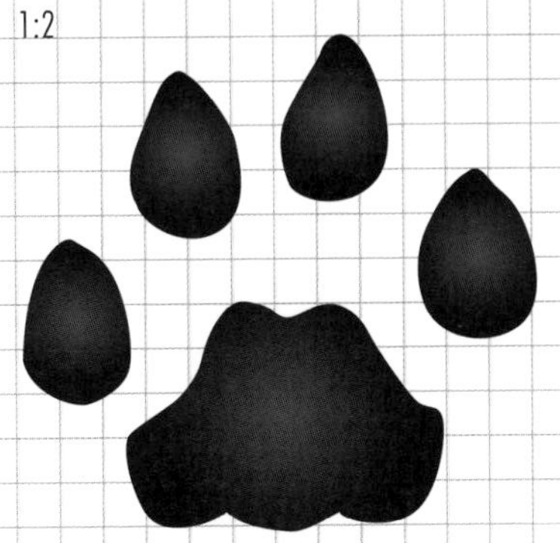

PUMA

SCALE
1:1.5

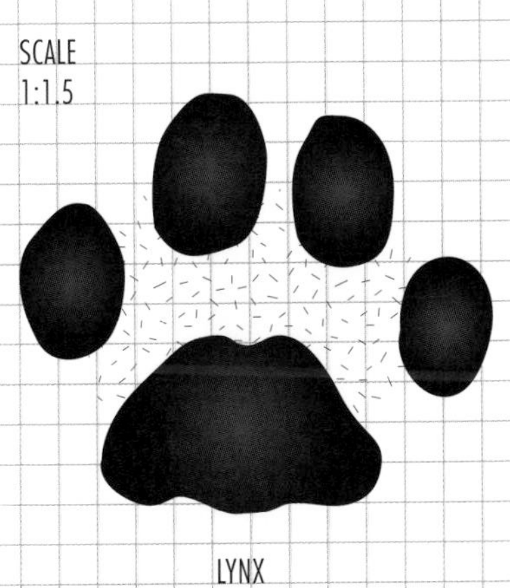

LYNX

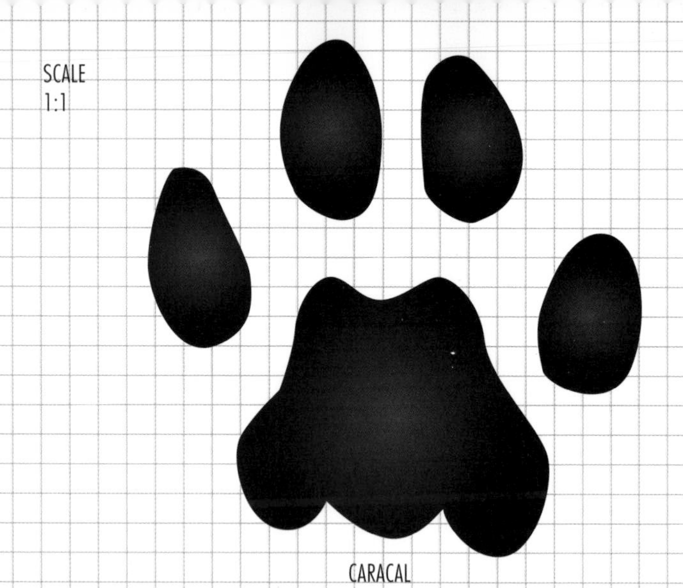

CARACAL

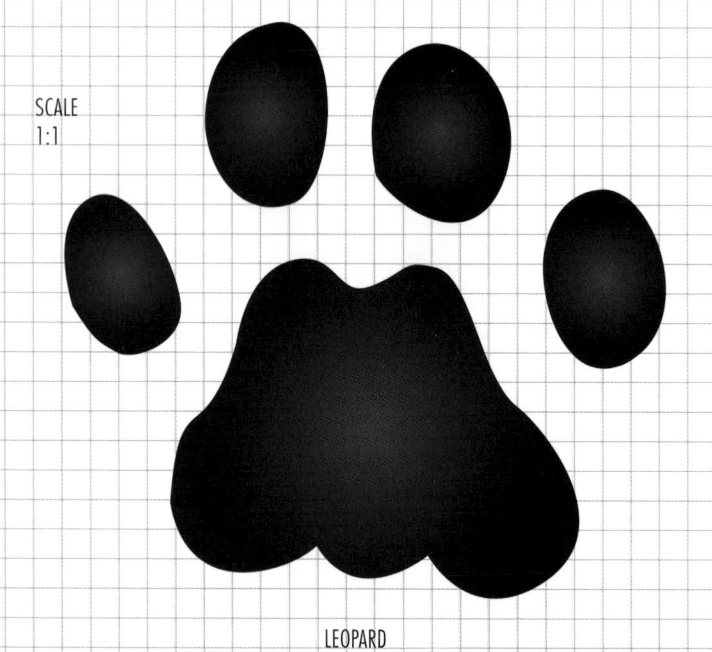

LEOPARD

SCALE
1:1

DOMESTIC DOG

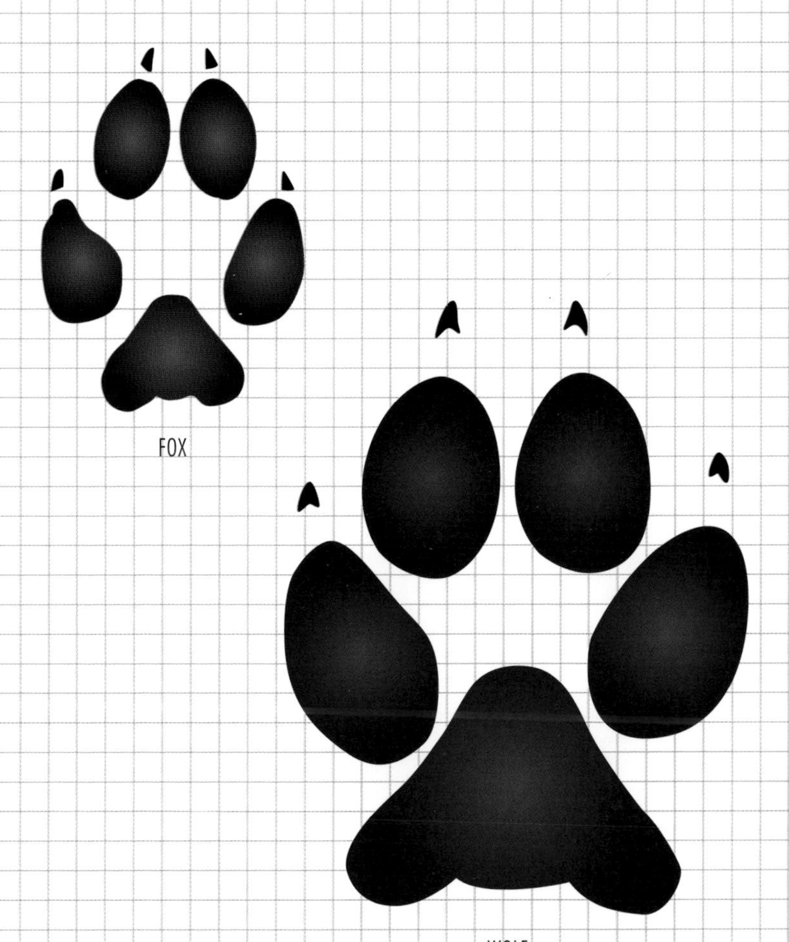

FOX

WOLF

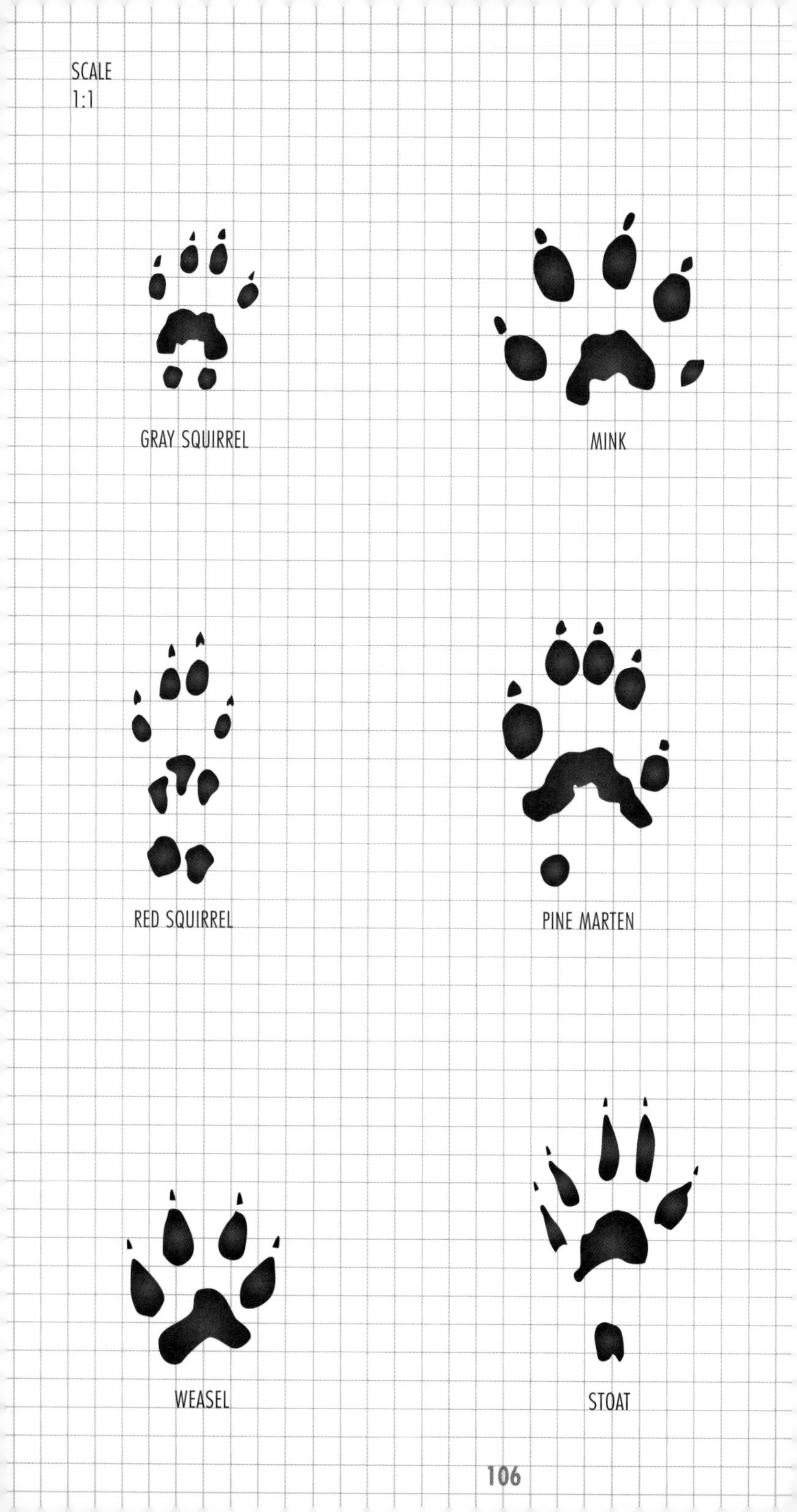
SCALE
1:1
GRAY SQUIRREL
MINK
RED SQUIRREL
PINE MARTEN
WEASEL
STOAT

SCALE
1:1

OTTER

RABBIT

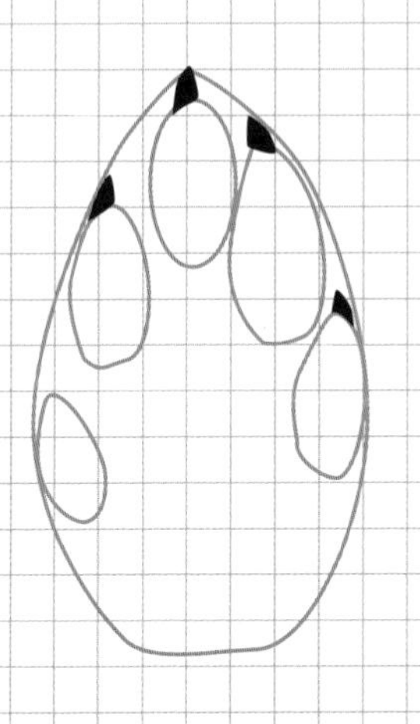

HARE

BADGER

SCALE
1:1
HEDGEHOG
HOUSE MOUSE
WATER VOLE
SHREW
RAT
SCALE
VARIABLE
TOAD
FROG
LIZARD
SNAKE

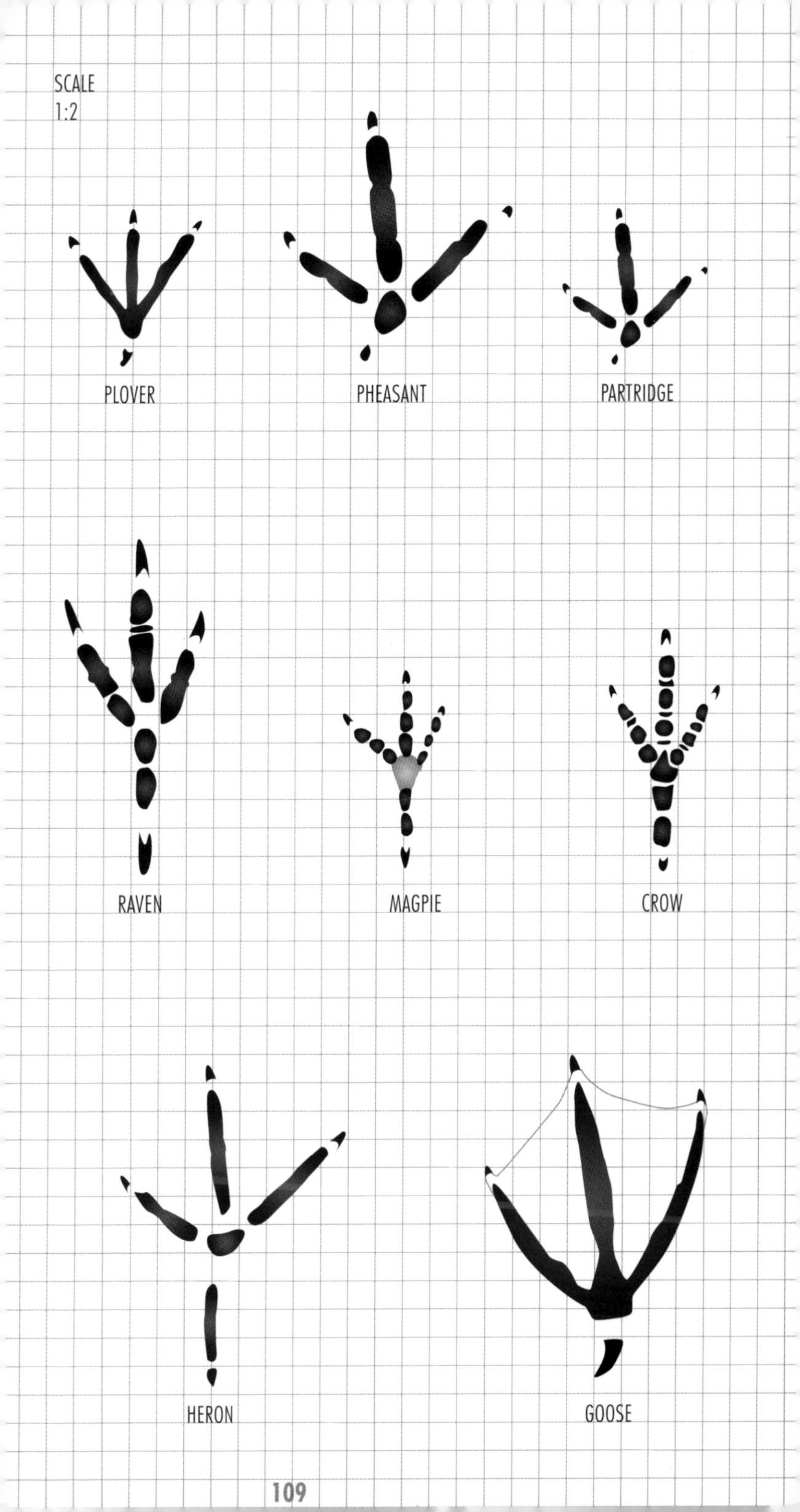
SCALE
1:2
PLOVER
PHEASANT
PARTRIDGE
RAVEN
MAGPIE
CROW
HERON
GOOSE

INDEX

ACKNOWLEDGMENTS
With special thanks to Rhoda Mcgivern and Daniel Rasmussen.

PICTURE CREDITS
The publishers would like to thank the following for the use of their images featured in this book:

Jupiter Images: 13, 48, 49, 50, 51, 54
iStockphoto: 1, 2, 24-26, 28-30, 32-40, 42-47, 52,
53, 55-61, 66-72, 75-87
FPLA Images: 62, 63, 64, 65, 74